Ciara Mulcahy

Maths
Displays

THÉRÈSE FINLAY AND
JACQUIE FINLAY

AUTHORS THÉRÈSE FINLAY AND JACQUIE FINLAY

EDITOR SALLY GRAY

ASSISTANT EDITOR LESLEY SUDLOW

SERIES DESIGNER LYNNE JOESBURY

DESIGNER RACHEL WARNER

ILLUSTRATIONS GAYNOR BERRY

PHOTOGRAPHS MARTYN CHILLMAID

The authors would like to thank St Laurence's RC Primary School, Wirral and St Winefride's RC Primary School, Cheshire for letting them set up their displays

Designed using Adobe Pagemaker

Published by Scholastic Ltd, Villiers House, Clarendon Avenue, Leamington Spa, Warwickshire CV32 5PR
Text © Thérèse Finlay and Jacquie Finlay

© 2000 Scholastic Ltd
6 7 8 9 0   5 6

British Library Cataloguing-in-Publication Data
A catalogue record for this book is available from the British Library.

ISBN 0-439-01636-3

The publishers gratefully acknowledge permission to reproduce the following copyright material:
Irene Rawnsley and John Foster for the use of 'Monkey babies' from *Blue Poetry Paintbox* ed. John Foster © 1991, Irene Rawnsley and John Foster (1991, Oxford University Press).

Contents

MATHS

Introduction

The importance of display

Displays are a necessary and crucial element of any early years setting. They provide an ideal opportunity to promote learning across the curriculum. They can be used flexibly, either as a stimulus to new learning or as a record of previous work undertaken. All children flourish through praise and encouragement and a sense of achievement. Display is the ideal medium in which to achieve this. It is essential that we demonstrate and celebrate the value of young children's work and as a result we develop their self-esteem.

The mathematical displays in this book have been devised for early years practitioners to use, whatever their level of confidence, experience and artistic expertise! They offer step-by-step, timesaving guidance and the varied range of displays for each sub-topic demonstrates how to achieve, interesting and lively displays within any setting.

The ideas in this book have been closely linked to the Early Learning Goals published by the Qualifications and Curriculum Authority. The Early

Introduction

Learning Goals divide the curriculum into six main areas – Personal, social and emotional development; Language and literacy; Mathematics; Knowledge and understanding of the world; Physical development and Creative development. All these areas of learning can be approached through a range of structured, imaginative, and free-play activities which all eventually prepare for the subjects of the National Curriculum.

The displays and activities within the book will provide a good foundation for the curriculum that children will follow once they are in school. They will also fit well into the pre-five curriculum guidelines issued by local authorities throughout Scotland.

Using this book
Themes on Display – Maths contains five chapters on the sub-themes of Colour; Number; Size, Position and time; Pattern and shape.

Each of these chapters develops an awareness and understanding of mathematical concepts, in an exciting and imaginative way.

In each chapter of the book the mathematical theme is introduced through a stimulus display to motivate and engage the children's interest. Once a firm foundation has been laid through the stimulus display, it may be followed up with the five interactive display ideas which will build upon the children's knowledge and understanding.

Each of the interactive displays is covered in detail and is presented on a double-page spread with colour photographs. The displays provide the children with a range of experiences and opportunities to further their mathematical and cross-curricular development.

It is important that children are provided with concrete experiences to enhance their mathematical learning and as a result there is a table-top display to conclude each chapter. These table-top displays provide the children with opportunities to develop the concepts in a multi-sensory manner.

Each interactive display in the book follows a set format using the following headings:

Title and Learning objective – All of the displays have a title incorporating

the theme of the chapter. Generally this is prominent on the display, depending upon size, space and relevance. A learning objective is also outlined to highlight the purpose of the display.

What you need – This provides a complete list of the resources necessary for completing the display. There is a broad range of readily accessible materials used within the different displays. These resources are not conclusive and appropriate substitutions can be made.

What to do – In this section there is a step-by-step guide to support the busy practitioner.

Talk about – This section provides a set of useful questions and suggestions designed to encourage the children to further their knowledge and understanding of the topic. These suggestions should help encourage all the children to actively engage in developing their ideas and expanding their mathematical vocabulary.

Home links – As parents play a vital role in their children's education this section provides invaluable ways to involve the parents. This may take the form of continuing work already started, gathering information or bringing things from home.

Using the display – A crucial element for each of the displays is how they can be used efficiently to cover different aspects of the curriculum. It is essential that the displays are used to the full and are not simply something to fill a wall space. The displays described in this book are intended to help fulfil our aims of providing a broad and balanced curriculum.

Although this book specifically focuses on mathematical learning, the displays are cross-curricular and may be used to cover all the Early Learning Goals. Although specific examples are given, a certain amount of flexibility is required, and most of the activities may be easily adapted for different levels of ability.

Aims of display

The following list is a summary of some of the different aims for creating stimulating displays:
● to provide a record of achievement or reference for the children's learning
● to create a stimulating environment and a purposeful working atmosphere where the children feel secure and confident
● to create a good impression for visitors
● to demonstrate that all the children's contributions are valid
● to widen the children's vocabulary through discussion and interaction
● to use an integrated approach to learning, providing broad and balanced learning opportunities
● to develop observational and manipulative skills as children create and interact with the displays
● to enhance personal and social skills through co-operative group work.

Interactive displays

Each chapter in this book contains five main interactive display ideas. Displaying children's work encourages them to appreciate and value their own efforts as well as those of their peers. It is essential that displays form an active part of learning. Once the children are able to interact and use the display, rather than just look at it, their learning is extended.

Encouraging the children to become involved in the displays can be achieved in many ways, and by using a variety of materials. The following are some suggestions:
● Use Velcro, cup hooks and curtain hooks to move objects and pictures around displays, either independently, or on the instruction of an adult.
● Add moveable parts or labels to displays to directly involve the children in their completion.
● Place matching and lotto games on display tables to provide opportunities for the children to refer closely to the display as they engage in play activities, and to encourage the development of their mathematical language. Also, commercially-produced construction kits provide a simple method for children to extend their learning and develop all areas of the curriculum.

Introduction

THEMES ON DISPLAY for early years

● Task cards may be designed for the children to follow simple instructions and can be differentiated according to the children's mathematical needs.

Stimulus displays

The introduction of each new theme in the book is supported by a suggestion for an initial stimulus display, which provides the children with a focal point for learning. These displays can be developed in a variety of ways, for example, by the adult setting something up, or by asking the children to bring in contributions to add to a display. Other suggestions include:
● encouraging the children to bring a favourite book, song, poem or number rhyme to life
● taking photographs on a local walk to stimulate a response to patterns or shapes in the environment
● discussing familiar settings, themes or objects from home with a mathematical theme such as times of the day, shopping and numbers around them.

Stimulus displays can be as intricate or as simple as you wish – the priority is to stimulate discussion, introduce new vocabulary and engage the children's curiosity.

Display tables

As a conclusion to each chapter, ideas for display tables linking to the main theme are presented. These are relatively simple displays, which relate to work undertaken on the mathematical theme. Display tables provide opportunities for the children to do some practical work to develop their mathematical concepts. Ideas for colour work include a display of coloured boxes, see 'Boxes of colour' on page 24 and ideas for pattern work include, 'Jewellery patterns' on page 60, where the children use coloured beads for pattern making.

Space everywhere!

In an ideal world, displaying the children's work should be relatively easy – with large, low-level pin boards available. Realistically, very few areas fit this scenario and it is therefore important to use all the available space imaginatively. The ideas in the book reflect the reality, and there are displays that have been positioned on a range of sized boards, walls, around awkward spaces such as sinks, doors and corridors. Displays should be a mixture of 2-D and 3-D work, and suspended at different heights to add interest. Displays, no matter how big or small, should always be meticulously planned.

Planning displays

All types of display, whether they be a stimulus, interactive or table-top display, need to be thought about carefully. Vibrant displays that surround the children enrich their learning and help to create a visually stimulating environment. When planning displays, a good tip is to consider the general mathematical theme or area that you want to do a display on. Next, determine whether you want the display to introduce a given area, consolidate the children's work or act as a reference for future learning. Then consider what space is available and where it will be positioned. Decide whether the children will be able to touch it and read it for themselves or simply be able to use it for reference. Then decide the materials to be used – what is available, what can be made and what is most

suitable. Finally, consider how the display can be made interactive.

Throughout these different planning stages, it is essential that the children are involved to encourage their co-operation and teamwork – their ideas and suggestions will often surprise you.

2-D and 3-D displays

Children live in an exciting technological world and need to be stimulated by vibrant interactive three-dimensional displays. Traditional or more formal displays can, through some simple methods, be revitalized to appeal to all children. Below are some suggestions.

To give depth to displays, attach cardboard shelves to the wall to project the display outwards. These shelves could be used to sit figures on, place task cards on, or hold moveable sections of the display. To add variety they can be painted, draped with material or covered with paper.

Attach folded pieces of card to the back of letters or objects to produce a raised effect. Other ways to achieve this effect include leaving raised sections or using a pleated effect instead of simply stapling a picture or object to the wall.

When constructing table-top displays, ensure that they have shape and form to add interest. Achieve this by placing boxes and containers of different shapes and sizes on a table or a cupboard top and covering with fabric.

Fabric and drapes

The secret of making displays attractive is to use the most effective materials. If possible, have a range of fabrics to hand. Fabrics are versatile and can be used to represent elements of a display (ideas in this book include attaching fabric to produce a ruched effect representing the sky, the sea and the grass); to cover unsightly walls; to drape from a wall or link a display board to a table-top. It can be used as an alternative to paper and will enhance displays. In awkward areas where it would be difficult to attach backing paper neatly, fabric can be quickly stapled to produce a gathered effect. In these circumstances, pictures can be pinned rather than stapled to the wall. This method has been shown in 'Build a shape' on page 70.

Fabric is also cost-effective as it can be reused and take on many purposes. If you are lucky enough to live close by a factory outlet or remnant shop, bargains can be purchased. Old curtains and bedding may also be put to good use to cover large unsightly areas.

It would be useful within the collection of fabrics to have an assortment of colours, patterns, textures and prints ranging from a plain-coloured

Introduction

cotton fabric to a beaded multi-coloured shiny fabric. There is always the option of tailor-making your own drape to suit your display. For example, numbers could be written, shapes printed or patterns created. This may be done by using cotton fabric with pastels, paint, fabric crayons or felt-tipped pens. The fabrics used should complement the patterns, theme or colours within the display, such as the striped and spotted fabric used for the display table in 'Spots and stripes', see page 54.

Labelling
All displays should be supplemented with large, clear labels and captions completed by both adults and children. Lettering should take a range of forms and sizes, and like the children's work itself, should always be mounted or

framed on colours that complement each other. It is important to enhance the children's level of interaction by adding questions and tasks for them to complete. These should be worded simply but also used by other adults as a prompt to extend learning.

Word processors are an invaluable tool because they produce perfect labels in different sizes, fonts, colours and effects. As word processors contain a great number of fonts, you can generally find a suitable font to match the theme of the display. For examples, see the font used for the display 'Flower power' on page 50, it is a floaty, flowery font, compared to the bolder, more chunkier font, used for 'Animal patterns' on page 52. Special effects such as bending or wrapping text can also be achieved on a word processor.

Children should have access to a range of print for the displays. This includes making use of adults to scribe, and their own emergent writing. Encourage them to make labels or write captions using thick felt-tipped pens, with the adult scribing underneath where necessary. Writing materials and coloured card or paper can be situated close to the display for the children to label independently.

Display titles can also be cut out from letter stencils – these can either be mounted onto strips of paper, shadowed by adding a second cut-out letter, or used alone.

Aesthetic displays

The finished display should invite children to become actively involved – to use all their senses, to think, to talk, to raise questions, to feel proud of their achievements and to recognize elements of the display as their own. The following hints or tips will help to achieve this:

● Make a collection of appropriate books for reference and story.

● Use a range of colouring materials to suit the purpose such as pastels for bright vivid colours, felt-tipped pens for finer detail, paint for larger areas, crayons and so on.

● Collect and use interesting collage materials such as feathers, sequins, coloured gummed paper, tissue paper, polystyrene curls and so on.

● Provide natural materials on the display tables to stimulate discussion or to use for collages.

● Use reclaimed materials as a versatile and cheap commodity. They can be used and modelled for a range of purposes from spaceships to arks and animals. When using reclaimed materials, turn the boxes inside out and reassemble with masking tape.

● Use artefacts to provide a further talking point and also allow the children to make contributions from home.

● Use photographs of the children and the local area as a stimulus or a record of the children's work.

● Artificial lighting can be used to create shadows or highlight certain features.

● When possible, position displays to make the best of natural light, for example the display 'Deep blue sea!' on page 18 was positioned under a skylight to make the blue water glisten in the sunshine.

● Carefully trim all the children's work, using a guillotine to maintain a regular shape. Vary this by cutting out irregular or cloud shapes.

Frames, mounting and borders

It is important to plan the colour scheme of the display so that the finished product is colour co-ordinated. The background may consist of a plain vivid colour to create a strong dazzling effect or may be printed with sponges or objects to give a more subdued effect. Borders bought from popular suppliers come in a range of colours, sizes, shapes, patterns and textures and can totally transform the finished display. An ideal way of creating the perfect border is to encourage the

Introduction

children to make their own as in the 'What is two?' display on page 26, where the children have drawn the number 2 on strips of paper with different-coloured felt-tipped pens.

When mounting individual pieces of work, consider colour, shape and texture and try to arrange the work imaginatively to achieve the best effect. Single- or double-mount the children's work in contrasting colours. Ready-cut coloured mounts can be bought from all main suppliers and with carefully trimmed work, a pleasing display can be quickly and effortlessly produced. To enhance the work being displayed, try drawing a fine line on the inside edge of the mount.

An impressive but time-consuming alternative to mounting, is the use of frames. If using commercially-produced frames, attach the work with masking tape as this can be easily removed, enabling the frame to be reused.

Assembling displays

To assemble the display gather all the elements, including the completed sections, resources and fixing materials. A staple gun is useful for attaching the backing paper but remember that these have to be removed at some point – so

don't use too many or press too hard!

To begin, arrange the completed sections with Blu-Tack or drawing pins to ensure the display is aesthetically pleasing. Once satisfied with the arrangement, attach them more firmly with a staple gun.

Displays can be used in a number of ways – on the back of a door, see 'Colourful colours' (page 16); on a free-standing board, see 'Building patterns' (page 49); on the back of a cupboard, see 'Find a shape' (page 61); as a moveable display see, 'Build a shape' (page 70).

Wherever displays are positioned they need to be versatile, attractive and user-friendly. It is also important to consider safety when positioning displays.

Resources

For each display in this book there is a list of resources. It is useful to keep a set of the commonly-used resources in a toolbox or basket. A checklist could include: scissors; sticky tape; glue; staple gun; stapler; staples; Blu-Tack; masking tape; double-sided tape; pencils; fishing wire; cup hooks; butterfly clips; fabric; paper-clips; drawing pins; glue gun; ruler; craft knife; staple extractor; pliers; Velcro; markers; pins; eraser.

Colours

I can see a rainbow

Learning objective: to learn the colours of the rainbow.

What you need
Rigid garden netting with large holes; card; variety of coloured and textured materials in rainbow colours; pictures of rainbows; stapler; scissors; cotton wool; grey tissue paper; gold foil; glue; white card; hooks and fishing line (adult use).

What to do
Show the rainbow pictures to the children and ask them to name the colours and describe the shape. Explain that they are going to make their own rainbow by weaving strips of coloured material through the garden netting.

Cut the netting into a rainbow shape and the material into strips. Show how to weave the material into the netting: 'in and out' or 'up and down'. Invite the children to take turns to weave pieces of material through the netting.

Once complete, wind appropriate coloured fabric around the edges to give a smooth finish. Cut two clouds from white card, cover one with cotton wool, the other with grey tissue paper. Attach a 'sun' covered in gold foil. Label the rainbow colours and staple the labelled clouds to either end. Suspend the finished rainbow from hooks screwed into the ceiling using fishing line.

Talk about
● When can you see a rainbow? Does the sun have to shine? Are the colours always in the same order?

Home links
● Encourage parents to visit DIY shops with their children to see the variety of paint colours and collect colour charts.

In this chapter you will find new and exciting ways to deliver and expand the topic of colour. Interactive, stimulating and inspiring display ideas include exploring 'hot and cold' colours, looking at colours in the local environment and mixing an artist's palette of colours.

Colours

THEMES ON DISPLAY for early years

Hidden objects

Learning objective: to match and recognize colours.

What you need
Single coloured pictures such as a red post-box; a blue bluebell; a yellow sun; a green apple and so on; a range of tissue, crêpe, Cellophane and sugar paper in red, blue, green, yellow, white and black cut into strips; large sheets of poster paper (one each of colours listed above); paint; brushes; scissors; glue; coloured netting; stapler; Blu-Tack.

What to do
Show the children the range of coloured papers asking them to name each of the colours. Sort and match the strips and stick them to the large sheets of poster paper. Throughout the activity reinforce the matching and naming of colours.

Staple large sheets of poster paper to the display board to create blocks of colour. Cover these with netting in corresponding colours to form pockets.

Now introduce the pictures in turn, asking the children to name the colour and object. Once the colour has been established, ask them to suggest other items of that colour such as a red apple, a red post van and red cherries.

Explain to the children that they are going to draw and paint a picture to match one of the coloured blocks on the display board. Let the children work individually to each complete a single-coloured painting. When the pictures are dry, invite the children to place them onto the corresponding block of colour.

Once the display is completed, table-top activities could be placed in front of the display board for the children to use including the following.
● A coloured checkerboard with a basket of small coloured objects to match to the base board.
● Make a speckled log, a pool and five frogs. As the children sing the rhyme 'Five little frogs', from *Apusskidu* (A & C Black), encourage them to move the frogs from the log to the pool asking – When are they camouflaged? How are they camouflaged? What colours can you see?
● Use thin strips of tissue paper in yellow, green and brown to represent sand, grass and mud. Place small colour cards of yellow, green and brown and a collection of soldiers by the side. Encourage the children to turn over a card and place the soldiers in that coloured tissue. Which makes the best camouflage? What colour clothes would the soldiers need to wear to hide in the sand?

Talk about
● Discuss with the children

what happens when a red apple is placed on a red background. Why is it difficult to see?

● Introduce the idea of camouflage to the children, asking them to think of different examples such as soldiers, animals and insects. Explain how soldiers going into battle wear green clothes and paint their face and hands with muddy colours to help camouflage them. Chameleons and stick insects protect themselves from other animals by disguising their appearance or colour.

Home links
● Ask the children to find out the favourite colours among the members of their families.
● Invite the children to bring in coloured objects from home to add to the display.

Using the display
Language and literacy
● As a group, make labels for each of the colours. Ask the children to read the labels and place them with the correct colour.
● Provide strips of paper for the children to make lists of the objects hidden in each section.
● Organize a group visit to the local library to look at story or picture books about camouflage. Share and discuss them together.

Mathematics
● Ask the children to count and label the number of objects hidden in each section. Encourage them to write the number using the same coloured felt-tipped pen.
● Take away some of the pictures and ask the children to count how many objects are left.
● Ask each child to choose a wooden block in their favourite colour. Make the blocks into towers to discover which is the most popular colour. Transfer this information onto a bar graph to discuss with the children.
● Challenge the children to count the items in two blocks of colour as a beginning for practical addition work.

● Discuss with the children ways of sorting objects other than by colour, such as by size and type.

Knowledge and understanding of the world
● Encourage the children to think of coloured objects in nature that do not change colour, such as a dandelion is always yellow. Use photocopiable page 73 to develop understanding of the colours of the environment. Ask the children to colour the objects in appropriate colours.
● Investigate with the children the objects on display. Where are they found? Are they living or non-living? Who would use them? What are they made from? Are they natural or manufactured?

Creative development
● Encourage the children to use percussion instruments to represent the colours on display for example quiet, gentle sounds for green, compared to loud, banging sounds for red.
● Provide the children with circles of card, pencils and colouring materials. Invite them to make colour spinners. Ensure adult help is available.

Colourful colours

Learning objective: to recognize colours and the way the colour names are written.

What you need

Paint; paintbrushes; blue backing paper; large white card; glue; scissors; staple gun; wool; oil pastels; envelopes; sponges; painting pots and trays; selection of paper in shades of green; egg box; pipe-cleaners; Velcro; small piece of coloured fabric; sewing materials; two cardboard tubes (one very tall); coloured writing materials.

What to do

Explain to the children that they are going to use the door of your room to make a colour display which will help them to recognize the names of the colours and how they are written.

Tell the children all the things that they will need to make the scene. Let them work in small groups to produce these elements:

● a large painted yellow sun;
● sponge-painted grey clouds;
● a painted red post-box and lid made from a large piece of bent card;
● clumps of green grass in different sizes;

● someone walking (draw around a child in a walking position), painted in different colours with a detachable cap;
● a tree-trunk painted brown and leaves collaged with shaded green paper;
● a spider made from an egg box painted black and pipe-cleaners for legs;
● a butterfly using a cardboard tube and card painted wings;
● a coloured bag (made from fabric) to carry coloured letters for the children to post;
● a bus-stop – paint a large cardboard tube and label.

To assemble the display cover the door and surround with blue backing paper. Cut a rectangle in the post-box for the letters and make a 2cm fold down each side. Staple along each fold to ensure the post-box protrudes from the door. Place the lid on top of the post-box and staple to the door. Once in place, attach a cardboard base to the box and cut a flap for the children to retrieve letters.

Now staple the other items to and around the door, except for the cap, butterfly, spider and clumps of grass and the written colour words which will be attached to the display with Velcro. Position the tube to represent a bus-stop, add Velcro to the tube to store the words, pictures and task cards that will be used on the display.

Talk about
● Are spiders always black? What other animals could we add to the display?
● Can you think of some objects that are always the same colour? What objects, other than a post-box are always red?
● Do you have a cap? When would you wear a cap? What colour is it?

Home links
● Ask parents to take their children on a walk to post a letter and explain the writing to them that is on the front of the post-box.
● Ask parents to reinforce colours with their children when they are out – colour of cars; colours in nature; colours in shops, and so on.

Using the display
Language and literacy
● Provide opportunities for the children to write a letter or draw a picture – with help they should address an envelope and post the letter to themselves.
● Encourage the children to label the display.
● On coloured paper, make written or pictorial lists of objects in that colour.
● Encourage the children to match the words to the colours on the display.

Mathematics
● Make coloured letters for the children to post in sequence following a task card. Differentiate task cards by using colours, colour and word, and word only.
● Using the display as a reference, one child should name a colour and another name the corresponding object on the display.

Knowledge and understanding of the world
● Invite a postal worker into your setting to talk to the children about their job.
● Telephone the Post Office Education Service on 01795-426465 for a catalogue and to order the 'Lenny the Letter' videos, which describe the journey of a letter and provide additional related information.
● Discover and talk about with the children what other different colours butterflies can be.
● Look at trees and discuss with the children if they can tell which season it is by the colour of the leaves.

Creative development
● Make symmetrical butterflies using paint and folded pieces of paper.
● Use wax crayons and thin paper to make rubbings. Can the children guess each other's objects?

Colours

THEMES ON DISPLAY for early years

Deep blue sea!

Learning objective: to recognize the colour blue.

What you need

Blue material; blue and white tissue paper; raffia; glue; sticky tape; black marker pen; fishing line; hole-punch; bubble wrap; card; blue tablecloth or cover; set rings; blue card; blue items; writing and colouring materials.

What to do

Attach blue material to the ceiling, allowing it to hang as a backdrop for the fish. Bend the raffia into two large fish shapes and several smaller ones, securing with sticky tape. Glue white or blue tissue paper over the fish frames to form a base for the children to stick tissue paper on. Encourage the children to work in groups sticking and layering circles of blue tissue paper onto the large fish to create scales. Repeat this on the other side of the fish.

Ask individual children to work on the smaller fish by tearing strips of blue tissue paper and sticking them onto the frame. Once the fish are completed add black eyes with a marker and suspend at different heights from the ceiling with fishing line. Thread long strips of the bubble wrap onto the fishing line and intermingle these with the fish to create a watery effect.

Place a table covered in blue material under the display, provide set rings, patterned blue fish (made from card and showing different patterns such as zigzag, horizontal and vertical) and any available blue objects for the children to sort. Make appropriate labels for the table-top activities and ask the children to write captions for the display.

Talk about

● Where do fish live? Do they have to live in water? What happens to a fish if it is out of the water for a while? What other animals live in the water?
● Where might you find brightly coloured fish? What colours or patterns might they be?
● Have you ever eaten fish? What did you like/dislike about it? Are there many bones in fish?

Home links

● Ask parents to send in something blue for the children to add to the display.
● Send a note home asking if any parents who go fishing could possibly bring in their equipment to show the children.
● Devise a simple questionnaire asking the children if they have any pet fish at home. If so, what colours are they? What are their special names? What are their pet names?

Using the display
Personal, social and emotional development
● Read the children the story *Rainbow Fish* by Marcus Pfister (North-South Books). Discuss the feelings and attitudes of the other fish towards the rainbow fish.
● Introduce the concept of 'feeling blue' – encourage the group to think of ways to help each other if someone is 'feeling blue'.

Language and literacy
● Make labels for the fish introducing the children to other other words to describe big and little, such as small, tiny, huge, large and so on.
● Compile a list of blue objects found on the display table.
● Make labels from folded card for the display table. Ask the children to take turns to place them on the correct object.
● Together write instructions of how to make the blue fish.
● Compose a 'blue rap' with the children by asking them what is blue and inserting a chorus line after three or four suggestions such as: 'Blue, blue these are a few'.

Mathematics
● Discuss the different-sized fish with the children, introducing appropriate mathematical language such as big, bigger, biggest and so on.
● Introduce the concept of spatial relationships by using the display as a focus. Ask questions such as: What is below the big fish? What is next to the blue elephant on the table?
● Provide the children with a fish outline for them to make patterns and use these to sort into sets.

Knowledge and understanding of the world
● Make blue glasses or binoculars using blue Cellophane and card or tubes. Ask the children what the display and other objects look like through them.
● Take the group to the local fishmongers to look at the different types of fish.
● Bring in a fish for the children to examine closely using their sense of smell and touch. Develop their descriptive vocabulary such as slippery, slimy, cold, shiny, wet and so on.

Creative development
● Print blue patterns onto fish shapes and attach these to rulers for the children to use as an aid when singing songs about fish.
● Encourage the children to draw pictures of blue objects and make a 'Blue book'.

Colours

THEMES ON DISPLAY
for early years

Artist's palette

Learning objective: to name, make and recognize a range of colours.

What you need
Selection of paints; finger-paints or chalk pastels in primary colours; paintbrushes; black backing paper; large white card; paper cut into circles; coloured mounting paper; old nail brushes; newspaper; tissue paper; paper plates; black fabric; Velcro; gold foil; PVA adhesive; scissors; magnets; coloured dice; palettes made from card; an artists palette or picture; stapler, paper-clips.

What to do
Introduce the children to the primary colours, (red, yellow and blue). Explain to them that lots of new colours can be created from these. Demonstrate how this can be done, using finger paints or pastels. Give each child a circle and place each of the finger-paints around the circle ensuring that they are a similar distance apart. Invite a child to dip their finger in a colour and move it around

the side of the circle to visit another colour. This may be repeated with a different child and colour, until all the colours have been used and new colours formed. Allow the children time to experience this individually on their circle of card.

Now, explain to the children that when artists are painting they use a palette to create new colours. Show the children the artist's palette or picture of a palette, telling them that they are going to make a large palette for the wall. Cover the wall with black backing paper and draw an outline of a palette on a large piece of white card. Divide the children into groups to work on different aspects of the display.
- Ask one group to paint the card-shaped palette with brown paint mixed with PVA adhesive to give it a shiny effect. Once painted, drag a nail brush through the paint to give a grained effect.
- Another group can stick pieces of white tissue paper onto six paper plates to produce a raised effect.
- Ask a different group to mix and paint

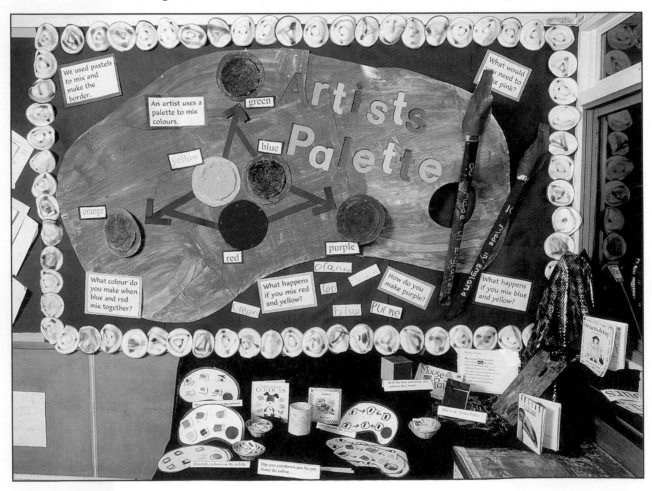

MATHS

Talk about

● Discuss with the children what an artist does. Introduce the concept of artists working with different media such as clay, charcoal and pastels. Tell the children that a sculptor makes 3-D works of art in stone, clay, metal, wood, and so on.
● What colours mixed together would make brown? What other substances could be mixed together to alter the original colour such as coloured jellies, coloured water and so on. Does the shade of the original colour make a difference? How could they make things lighter or darker?

Home links

● Ask parents to help their children to find examples of work by some famous artists.
● Inform the parents that their children are investigating colour mixing. Encourage them to point out primary and secondary colours in clothes, magazines and so on.

the tissue-covered paper plates using the primary and secondary colours (red, blue, yellow, green, orange and purple).
● Ask another group to make two paintbrushes by rolling pieces of newspaper into a paintbrush shape, painting, covering the end in gold foil and adding the 'brush' – made from painted brown card.

Once completed, attach the palette to the display board, pleating it to add depth and staple on the plates of colour. Make and staple black arrows to link up the colours, and staple the paintbrushes onto the palette. Mount the small circles of colour and use as a border.

Place the black fabric on a low level table in front of the display with the following resources and activity suggestions:
● Artists' palettes made from card with matching colour cards.
● Two dice showing the primary colours for the children to roll. If they are able to name the new colour made by mixing the two colours then they cover the colour on their palette.
● Paintbrushes with magnets on the end which the children have to dip into a pot of colours and words attached with paper-clips.

Using the display
Language and literacy

● Introduce alphabetical order to the children, give them two or more colours to place in the correct order.
● Discuss instructions with them, model reading and writing instructions for mixing new colours.

Mathematics

● Draw a snake with three segments onto a piece of paper. Photocopy it for each child. Supply coloured counters in the primary colours and ask each child to place two specific primary coloured counters at each end. Suggest that they use the display to decide what new colour should be placed in the middle.
● Using the paintbrushes and magnets, ask the children to take it in turns to dip for a colour or word and name it.

Physical development

● Look at a selection of pottery, encourage the children to make small pots using self-drying clay.

Creative development

● Show the children some work by an artist such as Jackson Pollock or Matisse who both use bright vivid colours.
● Ask the children to wear coloured bands for a dance session. Those wearing primary colours must move about the space and on a given signal find another primary colour. Extend this by asking the two children with primary-coloured bands to find the new colour that they would make together.

Colours

THEMES ON DISPLAY for early years

Fiery red, ice cool blue

Learning objective: to recognize and identify hot and cold colours.

What you need
Selection of pictures depicting 'hot and cold colours' such as beach, sunset, desert, summer, winter, ice or snow; coloured tissue paper; coloured paper; paint; black backing paper; red crêpe paper; blue and silver metallic paper; blue and red fabric; card; scissors; staple gun; glue; plastic shapes for printing; paintbrushes; palettes; Velcro; books and pictures about hot and cold places; labels.

What to do
Introduce the pictures to the children and ask them to sort them out. Encourage them to name the colours and discuss how they have sorted them. If necessary introduce the concept of 'hot and cold colours'.

Explain to the children that they are going to mix some paint to make a display of hot and cold colours. Divide the children into two groups. Provide red, yellow and white paint to one group, and blue, black and white paint to the other. Encourage the children to mix the paint on a palette and to experiment using different combinations of the various paints. Ask them to record the colours that they have made onto small pieces of paper.

Next, give the children the tissue paper to sort using the same criteria and challenge them to layer the tissue paper to give either a hot or cold effect. Frame the finished pictures to produce a professional finish.

Now, ask the children to paint hot and cold pictures using the original pictures as a guide. Mount the children's work on coloured paper to complement the colours in the painting.

Using paint, print circles in red, yellow and orange and thin rectangles in grey, pale blue and dark blue onto strips of white paper. Cut and mount the hot colours onto red crêpe paper in a wave border and the cold colours onto the blue metallic paper in a jagged border.

To assemble the display staple the black backing paper onto the display board, splitting it in half diagonally using coloured borders. Cut out the titles 'Fiery red' in bright red paper and 'Ice cold blue' in bright blue paper and staple them to the board.

● What colours make you feel cold? What happens when you are cold? What words could you use when you are cold?

Home links
● Ask parents to gather pictures of hot and cold countries from travel agents. Discuss particular features of these areas.
● Invite a parent to your setting to talk to the children about a hot or cold place they may have visited.

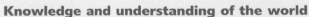

Using the display
Language and literacy
● Ask the children to describe the 'tube pictures'. An adult could scribe for them.
● Work with the children to create their own 'hot' or 'cold' poems.
● Use zigzags of card for the children to make their own 'hot' and 'cold' books.

Mathematics
● Use beads or cotton reels to make patterns from hot and cold colours.
● Make colour cards and show them one by one. Ask the children to name them and place them in the right 'pool' or 'fire'.

Knowledge and understanding of the world
● Investigate the climates of different countries.
● Set up investigations to discover the effects of heating and cooling on different substances such as water, wax and chocolate.

Physical development
● Show the children a selection of hot and cold colours, asking them to name them. Let them take turns to choose a colour and mime how they would feel such as blue – shiver, or red – fan themselves.
● Use play dough to mould animals from hot or cold countries.

Staple the small pieces of paper containing the mixed hot and cold colours onto the board at an angle to create a large 3-D effect. Staple the corners of the framed coloured tissue paper to give a raised effect, and finally attach the mounted paintings. Add the border and relevant labels to finish the display.

Once complete, place a table covered in blue and red fabric in front of the display. Include on it:
● Books referring to hot and cold places.
● Tubes painted red and blue to represent 'hot' and 'cold' colours. Attach relevant hot and cold pictures to the tubes using Velcro, such as a snowman, waterfall and river for the blue tube; a fire, volcano and sun for the red tube.
● 'A fire' made from card, covered in tissue, folded around into a cylinder and shaped into flames. A 'pool of ice' made from silver and blue metallic paper cut into a pool shape. These can be used to place suitable words in, such as: igloo, polar bear, flame and so on.

Talk about
● What colours make you feel hot? What happens when you are hot? What words could be used instead of hot?

Colours

Boxes of colour

Learning objective: to recognize colours and to appreciate that some objects always remain the same colour.

What you need
Kaleidoscopes; colour paddles; white material; scissors; glue; different-coloured Cellophane; card for circles and boxes; photocopiable page 74; blocks; modelling tools; home-made play dough (made with two cups of plain flour; one cup of salt; two cups of water; two teaspoons of cream of tartar and two tablespoons of cooking oil); pan; spoons; cup; cooker; board.

What to do
Copy photocopiable page 74 onto card and make into boxes. Glue different-coloured Cellophane into the 'cut-out' of each box. Make play dough, stirring all the ingredients in a pan over a gentle heat until the mixture leaves the side of the pan. Place the dough onto a board and knead until smooth.

Place blocks on the table to create different levels and cover with white material. Arrange made-up boxes, colour paddles and kaleidoscopes. Place the dough on the circles of card for the children to use, encouraging them to make fruit, shapes or animals. Invite the children to take turns to cover their shape with a coloured Cellophane box and discuss the new colour of their dough shape. Let the group investigate looking at different-coloured objects in the room through the colour paddles and encourage them to share their discoveries.

Talk about
● What makes the patterns in the kaleidoscope? Can they see every colour? Is the pattern better when they point the kaleidoscope to the light?
● What happens if you use two different-coloured paddles to look through? What would happen if you used different-coloured play dough?

Home links
● Ask parents to send in any interesting objects that could be placed in the colour boxes.
● Ask parents to collect boxes or kitchen rolls for the children to make their own colour boxes or binoculars.

Further display table ideas
● Make a specific colour table and ask the children to bring in objects from home.
● Discuss colours in nature, and create a table-top display that focuses on this idea, incorporating leaves, acorns, conkers, cones, feathers and so on.
● Talk about the colours used to represent danger – make a colour/danger display, incorporating traffic lights, road signs, safety helmets, fire engines and so on.

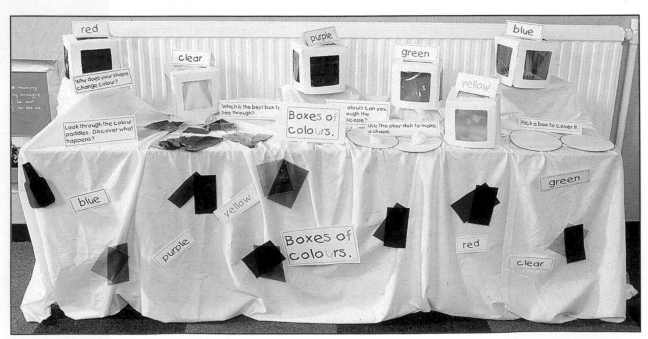

Numbers

Numbers from home

Learning objective: to recognize numbers around the home.

What you need
Selection of cardboard boxes and tubes; large sheets of coloured card; masking tape; sticky tape; assorted coloured paints; paintbrushes; paper; white fabric; fabric crayons or felt-tipped pens; egg boxes; sponge; scissors; craft knife; stapler; card; glue.

What to do
Open out the cardboard boxes into their net shapes, turn and reseal so that all colour and advertising are unseen on the inside. Use the boxes and masking tape to create a car, telephone and house. To make the house, use a large cardboard box for the base with card folded and attached with masking tape for the roof. Once complete, let the children paint it and add details using small pieces of card.

Make the telephone using two cardboard boxes of a similar size, attached together. Use a craft knife to cut the top box to shape and cover with card. Make a handset using a kitchen tube with egg boxes for the earpiece and mouthpiece and attach pieces of stiff card to the phone to rest it on. Cut small pieces of sponge for the buttons on the phone. These can be numbered and glued to the front of the phone.

For the car use two cardboard boxes, one bigger than the other, attached together, painted and with cardboard wheels glued to the sides. Ask the children to add finishing touches such as windows, lights and number plates made from card and felt-tipped pens.

On a piece of white fabric invite the children to write lots of coloured numbers, large and small, using either fabric crayons or felt-tipped pens. Use this to cover a table-top. Paint four strong tubes in bright colours and staple large sheets of coloured card to the tubes. Place the tubes on top of the fabric to create three sections. Put one of the models in each section. Provide the children with paper doors, cars and telephone dials for them to add their own numbers. Glue these to coloured card behind each model. Once completed add labels.

Talk about
● What is the biggest number you know? How do you know it is a big number?
● How many numbers are on a car registration? What number house do you live at? Do you know your own telephone number?

Home links
● Ask parents to provide telephone directories for the children to use and find numbers.
● Provide the children with a personal number book in which they can record numbers found around the home.

Spaceships, currant buns and teddies are all put to good use with the lively and inspirational display activities and designs in this chapter. Your number displays and tables will be brimming with interactive and tactile materials that will not fail to motivate and enthuse the children.

THEMES ON DISPLAY for early years

What is two?

Learning objective: to recognize and count to two.

What you need
Mod-Roc (use papier mâché if unavailable); newspaper; bucket of water; strong card; paint; paintbrushes; coloured paper; rubber gloves; coloured sugar paper; scissors; felt-tipped pens; glue; green backing paper; strips of white paper; string; thin cardboard tubes; stapler; cardboard boxes; sponges; red Cellophane; green crêpe paper; wooden plank; pairs of plastic animals; Velcro; *Two Shoes, New Shoes* Shirley Hughes (Walker Books); pictures of zips, buttons and bows; aprons; protective table covering.

What to do
Read *Two Shoes, New Shoes* to the children, asking them to think about what number they hear throughout the book. Demonstrate in a variety of ways

how to form a number two (in the air, on paper, in the sand tray, on their hand). Provide the children with strips of white paper and felt-tipped pens to write rows of twos both horizontally and vertically. These can be mounted onto black paper for the border. To produce the elements for the display, let the children work in small groups on the following activities. Ensure that the tables and children are suitably protected.
● Draw a large number two onto strong card and glue on newspaper to produce a raised effect. Dip strips of Mod-roc into water to cover the newspaper. Allow to dry, cut out and paint yellow. Double mount the number onto red and black paper.
● Stuff rubber gloves with newspaper, arranging the fingers into an open hand shape and cover with Mod-roc. Paint, mount and then frame.
● Draw two oval eye shapes onto strong card, add two circles for eyeballs using newspaper to create a raised

THEMES ON DISPLAY for early years

effect. Cover with Mod-roc, paint, mount, add curled black eyelashes and then frame.

● Draw two ear shapes onto strong card and cover with strips of Mod-Roc, layering sections to add definition. Paint, mount and then frame.

● Draw two lips onto white card, gluing scrunched-up red Cellophane in the outline. Once dry, cut around the lip shapes. Mount these on to white paper with a black centre and frame in yellow.

Now, ask the children to complete small drawings of all the above, using felt-tipped pens. Cut and double mount in red and black.

To assemble, cover the display board with green backing paper, arrange and staple the mounted work. Create an interactive section under the display board:

● Sponge print the background in blue.
● Staple a 'Noah's ark' made from reclaimed materials such as cereal boxes and card to it. Place a wooden plank for the animals to walk along in twos.
● Use tubes and string to create a washing-line for the children to hang articles in twos such as socks, T-shirts and trousers.
● Add a large coat, cut from card. Provide Velcro and pictures of zips, buttons and bows for the children to attach in twos.

Talk about
● Discuss the story *Two Shoes, New Shoes* with the children, asking them to name other things that come in twos, introducing 'pairs' to them, such as gloves, slippers, socks, wellingtons and so on.

Home links
● Suggest that parents allow their children to pair socks and gloves at home.
● Ask parents to help their children to practise forming the number two in different ways at home.

Using the display
Personal, social and emotional development
● Invite the children to find a friend to work with. In pairs, let the children copy one another, acting as animals.
● Ask the children to imagine themselves as Noah or one of his family in the ark. How would they feel? How would they look after the animals?

Language and literacy
● Use the story of *Two Shoes, New Shoes* as a starting point for the children's own poems.
● Tell the children the story of 'Noah's Ark' (traditional).
● Together, think of ways to describe the pictures on display such as two eyes, bright eyes or two ears, hairy ears.

Mathematics
● Use the selection of plastic animals to sort into different sets such as number of legs, colour, size and habitat.
● Place the animals in twos, encouraging the children to begin to count in twos.
● Make charts and graphs to represent eye colour.

Knowledge and understanding of the world
● Draw the outline of a child onto strong card, paint appropriately and cover with sticky-backed plastic. Cut into body parts for the children to remake like a jigsaw.
● Cut out facial features from magazines for the children to use for making 'funny faces'.

Physical development
● Encourage the children to carry out two of each action – skips, strides, hops, jumps and so on.
● Cut and stick simple 2-D shapes to create pairs of animals.

Creative development
● Teach the children the song 'Two' from the *Rainbow Songbook* by Eileen Diamond (International Music Publications). Add some appropriate actions.
● Make a playmat from sets of feet and hand prints on fabric in specific colours. Let the children follow a given pathway.

Higher and higher

Learning objective: to recognize large and small numbers, linking the concept that the higher the ladder rung, the bigger the number.

What you need
Number stencils; large cardboard tube; card; felt-tipped pens; scissors; glue; stapler; paint; paintbrushes; teddy bear outline; Velcro; large sheets of thick card; laminator or sticky-backed plastic; aprons and protective table covering.

What to do
Explain to the children that they are going to create a ladder and put numbers on it. If they were climbing a ladder where would they start? Where would they finish? What number would go on the bottom of the ladder and what would go on the top? Provide cut-out teddy bears for the children to colour for each of the numbers on the ladder. The children may decide how to decorate their teddy bear but need to realize that the teddy bears that are on the same rung like to look the same as each other. Organize the teddy bears, ensuring that there are sets to match the numbers. Once completed, provide the children with the number outlines, inviting them to decorate them in the

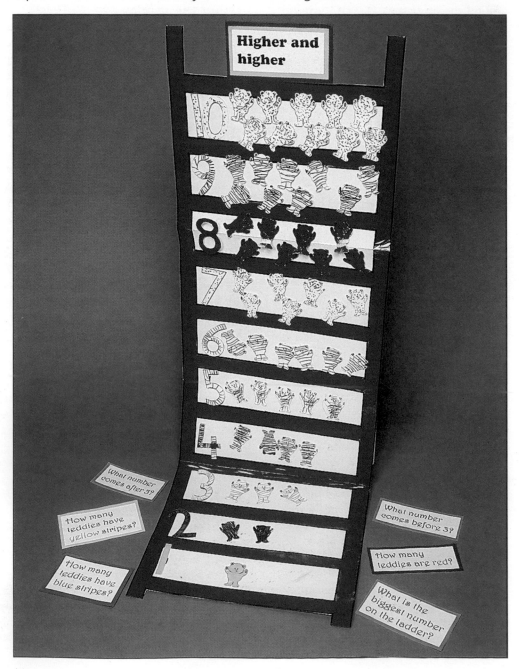

Using the display

Language and literacy

● Challenge the children to sort the teddy bears into families and devise names for them.

● Work with the children to decide on what the teddy bears may be thinking or what they are expecting to find at the top of the ladder.

● Provide the children with a speech bubble to accompany the bears. Ask them to write (or scribe for them) what they think the bears might be saying.

Mathematics

● Invite the children in turn to choose a number, deciding whether it is a high or low number. Ask them to position it on the ladder accordingly.

● Use all the teddy bears to sort by a given criteria, such as all the dotted teddy bears together.

● Use photocopiable sheet 75 to sort and match some teddies.

● Play a guessing game of 'higher and lower' using large numbers turned face down. The children take it in turns to guess if the next number is higher or lower.

Knowledge and understanding of the world

● Hide a teddy bear with some treasure to develop the children's ability to follow instructions and simple maps. Provide simple pictorial clues for the children to follow, such as under

the table, on the chair and in the cupboard.

● Choose a teddy bear to 'whisper' questions to you, such as, 'I am thirsty. Where can I get a drink?'. The adult repeats the questions to the children and asks for their suggestions. Ask individual children to take the teddy to the right place.

Physical development

● Collect together a selection of teddy bears to hide outside in a range of places. Challenge the children to go on a 'bear hunt' to find as many teddies as possible. Throughout the hunt describe different conditions for the children to travel through; such as rainy days and puddles or hot days and sunshine.

● Make individual teddy bears using card and butterfly clips to make them moveable. Decorate them with paint, felt, wool or collage.

Creative development

● Display a variety of teddy bears for the children to sketch, support the children through careful questioning.

● Make teddy bear masks with the children, wear these to a teddy bears' picnic.

same way as the teddy bears, for example – a red number one with one teddy bear to match; a blue dotted number two with two teddy bears to match and so on. Laminate or cover with sticky-backed plastic.

Paint a large ladder on the card, ensuring there is enough space for the numbers 0 to 10. Once dry, staple to a large cardboard tube. To complete, attach the numbers and teddy bears to each of the rungs with Velcro.

Talk about

● Discuss the different colours and patterns on the teddy bears with the children. How are they the same? How

are they different? Are any of the numbers decorated the same as the teddy bears? Why?

● Do you take a teddy bear to bed with you? What colour is it? How big is it? Does it have a name?

Home links

● Ask parents to play with their children, placing toys and teddy bears into family groups.

● Encourage the parents to count with their children as they get dressed, or tidy things away.

● Suggest parents have a number hunt to look for familiar numbers when they are out with their children.

Space race

Learning objective: to introduce the concept of first, second and third.

What you need
Variety of reclaimed materials; masking tape; sticky tape; glue; glitter; cotton wool; coloured and silver paint; paintbrushes; star-shaped sponge; coloured tissue paper; polystyrene balls; fishing wire; stapler; black backing paper; scissors; felt-tipped pens; white and silver card; coloured paper; butterfly clips; selection of plastic animals; vehicles and people to race; aprons; table covering; black fabric; 'Spaceship Race' by Charles Thomson (*Blue Poetry Paintbox* Oxford University Press).

paper to help secure the paint. Choose a single colour to paint each of the spaceships, using glitter to highlight specific features.

Use a star-shaped sponge to print silver stars onto the black backing paper. Once dry, staple this to the display board. Create a racing track by shaping strips of silver card to attach to the wall. At one end, roll up two thin paper tubes and staple them down. Make a 'Finish' line. Ask the children to paint numbers, in sequence starting at 0 on pieces of coloured paper. Glue onto the race track when dry.

Make planets by sponge-painting circles of card, painting polystyrene balls or joining rings of card to polystyrene balls. Staple these to the display or suspend them (using fishing wire). Staple down the 'crashed' partly-made rocket, adding puffs of cotton wool smoke.

Suspend the coloured rockets along the track in first, second and third place, using fishing wire.

Draw and paint rockets onto strong card, cut out, pinch and staple to the wall to give a 3-D effect.

Arrange objects on a table-top to develop understanding of ordinal number. Make an oval racing track from card, and position objects ready to 'race' such as cars, people or animals. Make a podium for the winners using reclaimed boxes. Make labels for the display.

What to do
Read the poem to the children, explaining that they are going to make a 'spaceship race' on the wall. Using the reclaimed materials, help them to make three different rockets and one partly-made rocket. Encourage them to use various joining devices such as glue, masking tape, staples or butterfly clips. Cover the finished models with tissue

Talk about
● When do we hear first, second and third? What do people receive if they come first?

Home links
● Ask parents to encourage the use of the words first, second and third, such as when taking turns in a game.

Using the display

Personal, social and emotional development

● Make first, second and third badges for the children to wear during the day, indicating who will line up first, play in the sand first and so on.
● Divide the children into small groups, providing each child with a hat and scarf. Challenge the children to compete to see who is first, second and third to get ready.

Language and literacy

● Make a microphone from a kitchen roll tube and egg box for the children to use to commentate on the race.
● Introduce new vocabulary such as 'whizz, zoom and whoosh' which describes the display and the speed of the rockets.
● With an adult acting as scribe, encourage the children to tell a story about an adventure in space. Encourage them to incorporate the new vocabulary.

Mathematics

● Using the table-top activity, encourage the children to 'race' the objects naming which came first, second and third.
● Use the race track as a number line to ask questions such as: Which number comes after 10? What is a big number? Which is the last number on the track?

● Count and label the number of planets and rockets.

Knowledge and understanding of the world

● With the children, find out information about space – what are the planets called? How many are there? Do they move?
● Talk about famous sports people and their achievements or those who were the first to accomplish something.

Physical development

● Devise simple races for the children to enter. Make rosettes for first, second and third.
● Play a game of 'Buses' by choosing some children to be buses. Give the others number cards with either first, second or third. The buses are to move about collecting 'passengers' in the correct order. Once the bus is full, the children can sit down. Repeat, choosing different children each time.

Creative development

● Use the book *Whatever Next!* by Jill Murphy (Picturemac) as a stimulus to develop the role-play area into 'space' using black fabric, corrugated card and items from the story.
● Introduce percussion instruments to use as you tell the poem. When the children are confident with the poem let them perform it for the parents.

THEMES ON DISPLAY for early years

Can you count?

Learning objective: to recognize and count from 0 to10.

What you need
Coloured A3 card; white card; A3 paper; glue; strong tape or string; plastic Christmas tree hooks; plastic-coated cup hooks; pastels; finger-paints; sponge numbers; scissors; hole punch; laminator or plastic covering; felt-tipped pens; paint; number stencils.

What to do
Tell the children that they are going to make a number line. Begin by drawing two sets of number outlines 0 to10,

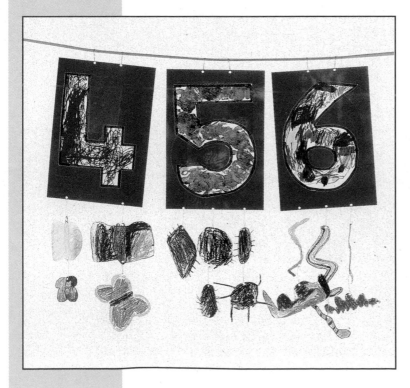

each one on an A3 piece of paper. Decorate both sets of numbers in a variety of ways, such as using finger-paints, felt-tipped pens or printing with sponge numbers or shapes. Cut out the numbers and mount both sets onto either side of the pieces of A3 card.

Ask the children to suggest different animals to be hung from each number, Provide small pieces of card for them to draw on and colour with pastels. Cut out the animals and colour both sides. Cover or laminate all the pictures and numbers. Punch holes into the numbers and pictures and hang them in the appropriate order.

Screw cup hooks and attach string or tape across the room to hang the numbers and pictures using the plastic Christmas tree hooks. Decide what height to display it at – low down so that the children can interact with it or high up as a point of reference.

Talk about
● Can the children count to ten forwards and backwards? Which is their favourite number? What animal is hanging from their favourite number? Which number is the same as their age?
● Where do we start counting? Where do we finish counting? Which is the largest/smallest number?

Home links
● Suggest some number rhymes to parents and ask them to recite them with their children.
● Ask parents to practise counting forwards and backwards with their children, such as when they are going up and down the stairs.

THEMES ON DISPLAY for early years

Using the display

Personal, social and emotional development

● Choose an animal from the display. Discuss which of the other animals would be their friend and why?

● Compare the eating habits of humans and other animals. Stress that humans should display manners.

Language and literacy

● Introduce adjectives to describe the animals. Play a game where the children guess an animal by its description.

● Make a big book with the children incorporating the animals from the number line.

Mathematics

● Share out the number cards asking the children to hang the numbers up in the correct order. Alternate this by changing the starting number.

● Hang a selection of numbers on the string. Ask the children to put those missing in the correct places.

● Introduce practical addition by hanging two different animals on one number.

● Introduce practical subtraction by removing a given number of animals from a number.

Knowledge and understanding of the world

● Discuss the different habitats of the range of animals.

● Conduct a simple survey to discover what types of pets the children have at home and how they look after them.

Physical development

● Use construction equipment to create a 'safari scene' for the animals from the display or make some animals from play dough.

● Play a game of 'Animal actions' with the children. Say a number from the number line and ask them to mime the movements or actions of the corresponding animal.

Creative development

● Listen to *Carnival of the Animals* (Saint-Säens) with the children and point out the different animals and the sounds that are used to represent them.

● Create a wall hanging by drawing or painting different animals onto fabric.

● Make a display of animals and their habitats with lift-up-flaps to reveal the animal, such as snakes under stones and birds under leaves.

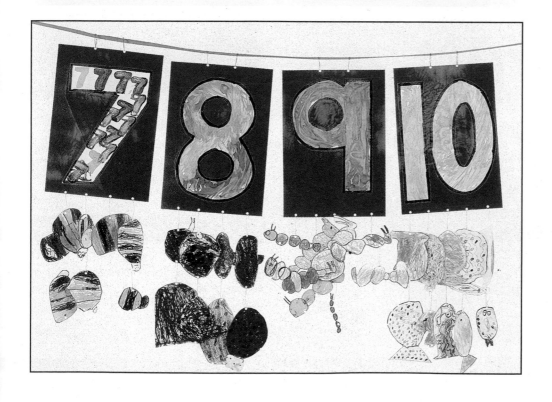

Five currant buns

Learning objective: to learn numbers through rhyme.

2 currant buns in a baker's shop,
Round and fat with a cherry on the top,
Along came a boy with a penny one day,
Bought a currant bun and took it away.

What you need

Coloured sugar paper; large pieces of paper; card; paint; paintbrushes; felt-tipped pens; laminator or sticky-backed plastic; sponges; shiny gold paper; the number rhyme 'Five currant buns'; pennies; baker's hat; buns cut from card; corrugated border roll; blue backing paper; scissors; staple gun; stapler; aprons; table covering.

What to do

Teach the rhyme 'Five currant buns' to the children, providing them with pennies, a baker's hat and five buns cut from card. Choose different children to pretend to be the baker, the buns and the customers. Repeat this activity several times, so that all the children take a turn. Explain to the children that they are going to create a display involving a baker's window, where they can go and buy currant buns.

Begin the display by providing five children with white A4 card to paint

buns, adding currants with black felt-tipped pens. Once dry, cut out the buns and laminate them. Ask other children to paint bread, jam tarts, rolls and so on for the other window.

To create shelves, ask the children to sponge-paint four long sheets of card and make the canopy of the shop by painting stripes on long sheets of card. Paint a door and a customer onto large sheets of paper.

To assemble the display, staple the backing paper onto the board and add border roll. Position the door in the centre using border roll to create a frame. Fold both long edges of the shelves, staple one fold to the wall, and leave a lip on the other to ensure that

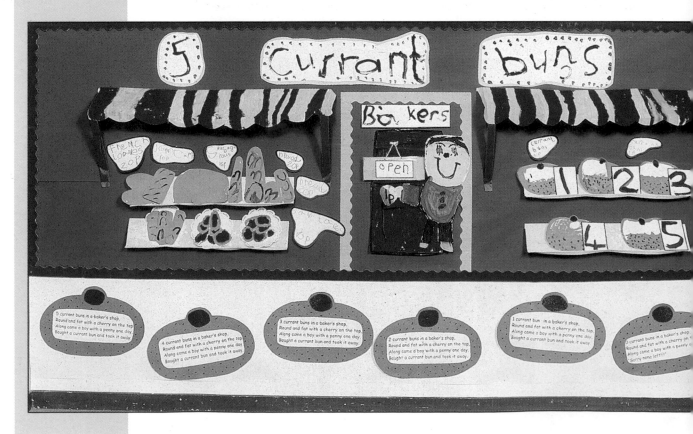

MATHS

the 'food' doesn't slip off the shelf. Fold one edge of the canopy and staple to the wall above the shelves. To ensure these remain in position add rolls of sugar paper to act as props.

Now, add the customer to the display, standing him or her in front of the doorway and attaching a penny for them to spend. Fill the shelves on one side of the door with currant buns and the other with the remaining food. Choose a child to paint '5 currant buns' to fit as a sign above the shop, and 'Baker's' for above the door. Ask the children to make labels and price tags to display alongside the food.

Attach the rhyme to bun-shaped cards to complete the display.

Using the display
Personal, social and emotional development
● Set up your role-play area as a baker's shop. Let the children make the food from play or salt dough. Stress to the children that they should be polite, use please and thank you, and remember to wait their turn and share when playing in the shop.
● Why do the children think it is important for people who work in a baker's shop to have clean hands, tied-back hair, hats, hair nets and clean overalls? Why do they use tongs to pick up the cakes?

Language and literacy
● Encourage the children to devise a shopping list for items that they could buy at the baker's.
● Record the children singing the rhyme onto a short cassette tape for others to listen to.
● Use photocopiable page 76 to develop pencil control and pattern-making skills.

Mathematics
● Use the display for practical addition and counting-on work.
● Introduce practical subtraction by counting the buns as they recite the poem.
● Introduce the value of small coins to the children.

Talk about
● What is a baker's shop? What do they sell? Where else can you buy these things from? What do bakers wear? Why? How can you make currant buns?
● What other types of shops do you know of?

Home links
● Encourage parents to take their children to a baker's shop to see what is sold there and perhaps to buy a cake or a bun.
● Ask parents to collect a variety of small coins for their children to play 'shopping' at home. Encourage them to label different items and to play 'shops' with their children.

● Make a graph to show the children's favourite sandwich fillings.

Knowledge and understanding of the world
● Follow a recipe to bake simple buns. Draw the children's attention to the properties of the ingredients before and after cooking such as texture, colour, form and so on.
● Discuss the changes in bread making. Explain that in the past it was usually made at home, but nowadays it is made in bulk and sold in supermarkets.
● Visit a local supermarket and buy a selection of breads from around the world – pitta bread, nan bread, soda bread, French bread and so on. Encourage the children to describe their appearance and taste, noting any similarities and differences.

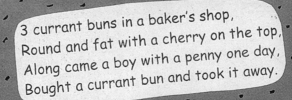

3 currant buns in a baker's shop,
Round and fat with a cherry on the top,
Along came a boy with a penny one day,
Bought a currant bun and took it away.

THEMES ON DISPLAY
for early years

Numbers, numbers everywhere

Learning objective: to know that large numbers exist.

What you need

Reclaimed cardboard boxes; paint; paintbrushes; shapes to print; large and small sheets of card; Blu-Tack; straws; felt-tipped pens; glue; cars; play people; scissors; masking tape.

What to do

Organize a short walk around the locality, asking the children to look out for numbers in the environment such as on doors, road signs, advertisements, cars, petrol stations and bus stops. Back inside, explain to the children that they are going to recreate a local scene using all the examples of numbers that they have found.

Create a base of paths and roads by painting and printing on large sheets of card joined together with masking tape. Invite the children to choose a box to represent a building which they have seen on their walk. Ask them to paint them with windows, doors and appropriate labels added.

Once the buildings are complete, position them on the base and provide small pieces of card for the children to write number signs and labels. Attach some of the signs to straws and stand them in Blu-Tack. Add extra details (such as playground games and car salesrooms) to reinforce the use of number in the environment. Place the cars and play people on the table-top for the children to play with.

Talk about

● Ask the children to suggest reasons why houses and cars are numbered. Why do shopkeepers and garages display the price of their goods?
● Can the children read any of the large numbers around them? Why are there numbers on road signs?

Home links

● Ask parents to point out different numbers in the environment when out walking or travelling with their children.
● Encourage parents to count groups of things when they are out with their children, such as blue cars, lampposts, bus stops and so on.

Further display table ideas

● Make a row of separate houses, each displaying a number. Place them on a street and use them as a focus for teaching odd and even numbers or to develop ordering skills.
● Make or provide some simple table-top track games for the children to play. Ask them to invent some of their own and display these.

Size, position and time

Place the monkey

Learning objective: to introduce and develop positional language.

What you need
A range of different-sized tubes; masking tape; newspaper; cold-water paste; dowelling; pipe-cleaners; brown paper; brown paint; paintbrushes; thick card; shades of green tissue and crêpe paper; scissors; glue.

What to do
Tape together three large tubes with masking tape to make a firm base – the 'tree trunk'. Now attach branches by adding thinner tubes at different angles and heights. You may need to secure these with pieces of dowelling. Attach the tree to firm card with masking tape so that it is free-standing. Help groups of children to dip sheets of newspaper into the cold-water paste. Drape over and around the tubes to create some texture for the bark. Leave to dry and then ask the children to paint the 'tree' with brown paint. Cut leaves from the selection of green paper and attach to the tree.

To make the 'monkeys', paint kitchen rolls brown, draw faces onto card and glue them on. Make arms and legs by folding brown paper concertina style. Staple a pipe-cleaner on for the tail.

Direct the children to hang the monkeys from specific places on the tree.

Talk about
● Explain that for the first few months of a baby monkey's life it clings to its mother's chest and then its back.
● Monkeys live in trees moving up and down them. How do monkeys move?

Home links
● Invite the parents to listen to the children reciting the poem 'Monkey babies' on photocopiable page 77, around the monkey tree.

MATHS

Fishy tale

Learning objective: to make comparisons between three objects using appropriate mathematical language.

What you need
Broadsheet newspaper; cold-water paste; stapler; paint; coloured paper; tissue paper; blue netting; white card; polystyrene chips; garden canes and dowelling rods; fishing wire; tin foil or silver paint; containers; reclaimed materials; ring magnets; paper-clips; fabric; a picture of people fishing; aprons; table covering.

What to do
Discuss the picture of people fishing, explaining to the children that they are going to create a fishing display. Begin by pasting together sheets of newspaper, overlapping them to form a rectangle 1.5m long. Make one more rectangle shape in the same way and leave them to dry. Choose a child to lie on the dry newspaper rectangles. Draw around them and cut out the shapes. Staple together the two 'body shapes' and pad with scrunched-up newspaper to form a newspaper figure. Invite the children to paint on clothes and features. In the same way, make the remaining two fishers, adapting them to measure 1m and 0.5m long.

Challenge the children to create three hats by dipping sheets of newspaper into the cold-water paste and draping them over three different-sized containers. Leave the hats to dry overnight and carefully remove them from the containers to let the undersides dry. Once dry, paint and position the hats on the fishers' heads – the smallest hat on the smallest fisher and so on.

Each fisher now needs a rod. Make three different-sized rods by painting silver or attaching silver foil to three sizes of garden cane. Add fishing wire to the rods and attach a ring magnet to each one. Make three ponds in different sizes from reclaimed materials. Paint the insides of the ponds blue and the exteriors green.

Using the display
Personal, social and emotional development
● Tell the children that fishers often take part in competitions to see who can catch the biggest fish. Discuss competitions with the children. What are they? Why do they have rules? Who enters them? Have they ever entered a competition?

Language and literacy
● Mix the labels on the display and invite the children to place them in the correct positions.
● Discuss the words on display. Draw the children's attention to the endings of the words. Encourage the children to generate similar words such as high, fast and so on.
● What do the children think the fishers are saying to each other. Scribe the children's suggestions. Laminate them and attach them to the display.

Mathematics
● Give the children a selection of coloured fish and numbers, asking them to place a set number of fish with the appropriate number card in each pool. Extend this to introduce practical addition using the three pools.
● Challenge the children to place a specific coloured fish in set places using the appropriate language of size such as place the blue fish on the long fishing rod, or place the orange fish on the short fishing rod.

Knowledge and understanding of the world
● Discuss the different places that fish may be found such as ponds, lakes, rivers and streams.
● Talk about which other animals live in water. Can the children tell you which animals live on land and which animals live in both.

To assemble the display, cover the display board with blue netting for the sky, attach green paper for the hills and add tufts of grass using green tissue paper. Decorate with flowers made from card and tissue paper attached to dowelling rods. Cut out three different-sized cloud shapes from white card and attach polystyrene chips. Create three small card shelves and cover with fabric. Position each fisher on a shelf, in size order, by stapling their legs to the shelf and their bodies to the wall. Attach the appropriate-sized rod to each of the fishers. Now place the three ponds on the floor, one in front of each fisher. Put an appropriate-sized fish, made from papier mâché in each pond. Attach a paper-clip to each fish.

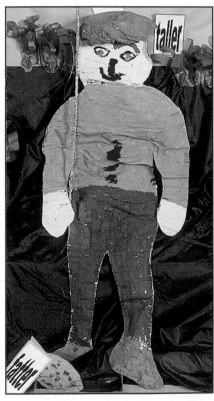

Label the display appropriately, using the language of size and comparison.

Talk about
Tell the children that there are many different types of fish and that they come in a variety of shapes and sizes. Ask the children to tell you who has caught the biggest fish. Try to use comparative language when asking the children questions such as: Has the tallest man got the biggest hat? Who is wearing the smallest hat?

Home links
● Ask the parents to discuss the family using comparative language. Who is the tallest? Who is the smallest/youngest? and so on. Ask parents to reinforce the use of comparative language at home whenever possible.

MATHS

Where is it?

*Learning objective: to develop an
understanding of position and related
language.*

What you need
Coloured paper; kitchen roll; egg boxes;
reclaimed materials; large sheet of card;
selection of collage materials including
feathers, wool, straw; paint; sponges;
paintbrushes; paper-clips; oil pastels;
concentrated dye; blue backing paper;
marker pens; cup hooks; curtain rings;
sticky tape; aprons; table covering.

What to do
Explain to the children that they are
going to create a display and use it to
describe where objects are placed. Invite
the children to work in groups to make
the objects (or similar objects) described
below.
● House – cut out a house shape from
card and provide the children with
marker pens to draw on windows,
curtains and bricks. Colour these with
oil pastels and wash over the top with
concentrated dye.
● Door – turn a cardboard box inside

out, cut a flap to create a doorway and
paint.
● Trees – draw and cut trees from card
and paint.
● Car – attach two cardboard boxes, one
bigger than the other, together. Paint the
boxes and glue cardboard wheels to the
sides. Add finishing touches such as
windows, using coloured paper.
● Bird – use a kitchen roll and egg boxes
to form a bird shape. Paint and add
feathers.
● Nest – cut out a nest shape from card,
paint and add wool and straw.
● Girl – use reclaimed boxes to create a
head and body for the girl. Make arms
and legs using rolls of paper and attach
them with paper-clips. Use collage
materials to add features and clothes.
● Dog and butterfly – use kitchen roll,
egg boxes and card to create a dog and
a butterfly. Paint and add features.
   Assemble the display by stapling blue
backing paper to the board and
attaching the house and trees. Sponge
print clouds onto the sky and attach
other features such as extra clouds, a
sun, grass, flowers and a path. With
sticky tape attach curtain rings to the car,
dog, girl, nest and bird.

Screw cup hooks into the display board for the children to hook the objects into different positions. For example place the car in front of the tree and the girl next to the house and so on.

Talk about
● Ask the children to describe what they would find outside their houses. Ask them to describe the position of specific objects. Would you find a car **in** the sky? Would you find a girl **on** a roof? What could be **up** a tree? Do you think you might find a cat **under** a fence?

Home links
Explain to parents that the children are learning to use positional language. Encourage them to discuss with their children, when they are out together, what they might see in a garden, beside a house, on a fence and so on.

Using the display
Language and literacy
● During circle time invite individual children to make up a story incorporating the objects on display.
● Encourage the children to use a variety of adjectives to describe the objects on display.

Mathematics
● Make simple task cards that direct the children where to place the objects. Leave the cards near to the display and encourage the children to work in pairs.
● Play a game together. The adult names the position of an object and the children have to work out what the object is.
● Invite the children to count and label the number of objects as they are placed on the display.

Knowledge and understanding of the world
● Talk about the variety of places that animals live in. Encourage the children to think about why different animals like different places.
● The display shows a picture of a house and garden. How might the garden look during the different seasons? Talk about the changing seasons and help the children to develop an understanding of the passing of time.

Physical development
● Using construction materials, encourage the children to build a similar scene to the one in the display. Ask them to move figures or a controlled toy around it in a specific sequence.
● Use apparatus such as benches, hoops and so on to create a simple circuit. Encourage the children to follow directions to move over, under, beside, onto or next to the equipment.

Creative development
● Develop a set of actions to mime the processes of building a house. Discuss the various tasks such as sawing, hammering, bricklaying and so on. Divide the children into groups and ask them to perform in sequence.
● Invite the children to paint pictures of their own homes. Use these to create a street scene.

Cor! What a size!

Learning objective: to introduce mathematical language.

What you need
Large sheets of card; paper; pieces of card; paint; paintbrushes; sponge; felt-tipped pens; pastels; tissue or crêpe paper; feathers; sand; sawdust; Artstraws; cotton wool; glue; stapler; scissors; wool; oil pastels; pictures of Noah's ark and animals; blue fabric; aprons; table covering.

What to do
Show the children the pictures of Noah's ark and the animals. Ask them to name and describe the animals, concentrating specifically on their size and shape. Explain to the children that they are going to create a big Noah's ark display with lots of different-sized animals.

Using the sponge brushes paint large sheets of card, some brown and others purple. When dry, paint black lines on several sheets of brown to create a wood effect for the base of the ark. Cut out a gangplank and a triangular 'roof' from the remaining brown card. Use a variety of techniques to paint the animals, such as following the suggestions below.

● Elephant and hippopotamus – draw and paint using grey paint mixed with sand or sawdust to create a rough texture.
● Birds and butterflies – draw and colour the bodies, gluing brightly-coloured feathers for the wings.
● Hedgehogs and spiders – draw the basic shape, glue Artstraws to form the spikes and legs. Use cotton wool to make the body of the spider.
● Crocodile – draw the long shape, glue thin paper over the crocodile to create a scaly texture and paint green, add teeth with card.

- Giraffe – draw a tall animal, paint and glue crêpe or tissue paper to form the markings.
- Snakes – draw and colour thin snakes using brightly-coloured pastels.
- Ant – draw the shape, glue cotton wool to the body and paint black.
- Ladybird – draw the shape and paint it red with black spots.
- Bees – paint a cardboard tube brown and yellow and glue wings using coloured card.
- Monkey – paint a monkey shape black and glue wool on it to look like hair.
- Ostrich – draw the basic shape, paint the correct colours and stick on pieces of concertined tissue paper to represent feathers.
- Peacock – draw the shape and glue coloured feathers onto the tail.
- Mr and Mrs Noah – draw and paint faces attaching cotton wool and tissue paper for the hair and features.

To assemble the display, cut and fold the brown card to form a lip and staple it so that it stands out from the wall. Staple the purple card over the top of a door or archway and cut an arch. Attach the roof and a gangplank to the side of the ark for some of the animals to walk up. Attach blue material for the water. Position the animals around the ark and Mr and Mrs Noah as though they are peering out of portholes to create the scene. Encourage the children to help you to label the display with the size of the animals.

Once the display is finished, place a stage block or climbing frame under the archway and let the children take a turn to stand in the ark. Remove the climbing frame once all the children have had a turn for safety reasons.

Talk about
- Discuss the story of 'Noah's Ark' together. Why did all the animals go into the ark? In the story, how many of each animal went into the ark? Which animals do you think would be friends? Would you like to live on an ark? Why?

Home links
- Ask parents to send in some pictures of animals for the children to use as inspiration for their creative work.
- Encourage the children to bring in a model animal from home to show to the group, and if possible, to leave next to the display.

Using the display
Language and literacy
- Tell the children the story of 'Noah's Ark'. Invite them to keep a diary of events from Mr Noah's viewpoint. Encourage them to include what happened in the story and how he felt.
- Play a game of 'I spy', using the ark and the animals.
- Make an animal book, with speech bubbles for the children to write the animal noise or a simple phrase for each of the animals.

Mathematics
- Sort a selection of small-world play animals into size and shape categories.
- Use pictures of animals, challenging the children to grade them in order of size such as tiny, little, small.
- Use small-world play animals to create a pattern such as plain and patterned; grey and brown; large and small and so on.

Physical development
- Ask the children to think about how they would keep fit if they were stranded on a boat for a long time. Use the suggestions for a 'fitness lesson'.

Times of the day

*Learning objective: to learn about time
in the context of familiar routines.*

What you need

Backing paper; border roll; paper;
selection of collage materials; glue;
stapler; scissors; string; drawing pin;
pencil; felt-tipped pens; egg timers;
stop-clock; plastic trainer clock;
cardboard clocks; books related to time;
aprons; table covering.

What to do

Talk about the different routines that
the children follow throughout the day.
Help the children to understand that the
routines of the day take place in a cycle,
for example one follows on from the
other and they are repeated every day.
Explain to them that they are going to
make collage pictures of the times of
the day and place them on a circle to
represent the clock face. Choose
individual children to decide their own
interpretation for each time of the day.
For example:
● *Morning* – getting up: collage a child
and clothes.
● *Morning* – breakfast: collage a bowl
and packet of cereal.
● *Noon* – eating lunch: collage and paint
a plate of food and cutlery.
● *Early evening* – eating dinner: collage
and paint a family sitting around a table.

- *Evening* – watching TV: collage two children watching television.
- *Night* – bedtime: collage a child asleep in bed.

Encourage the children to write a phrase for each time of the day.

To assemble the display, draw a large circle using the string, pencil and drawing pin (as a sort of compass). Cut and staple to the covered display board. Use the border roll to divide the circle into six equal segments. Staple the collaged pictures and phrases in time order, around the circle. Finish the display by providing clock faces for the children to colour in and add hands to, showing the appropriate times. Staple around the large circle.

Talk about
- Discuss the different events of the day together. Encourage the children to suggest what comes before and afterwards. Are there any events which happen more than once during a day?
- What things happen during the day time and during the night time? Do these change at different times of the year?

Home links
- Explain to parents that you are introducing the topic of time. Ask them to help by introducing the term 'o'clock', and by referring to clocks and watches at home.
- Ask parents to help their children to draw or write about something that happens at home in the evening.

Using the display
Personal, social and emotional development
- Adapt the words from the song 'Here we go round the mulberry bush' to include actions from different times of the day, such as 'This is the way we eat our lunch, eat our lunch' and so on.
- Ask the children to tell you about the routines that they follow in the morning. What do they do after they get out of bed? What do they do next? Do their routines always stay the same? Are they different at weekends?

Language and literacy
- Provide a notebook and a special teddy and let the children take turns to take it home. Ask the children (with the help of an adult) to write or draw the adventures that teddy had during the evening.
- Make a big book of day and night together. What animals can you see during the day? What animals can you see at night? Use pastels for the illustrations and add a simple, repetitive phrase for the text.
- Use telephones to develop speaking and listening skills. Encourage the children to pretend to speak on an answer machine, leaving a message and the time of their call.

Mathematics
- Take photographs of the children in action at different times during the day. Mount and laminate. Ask the children to place them in sequence.
- Look at the display and play a game with the children. Describe an event during the day and challenge them to name what comes before or after it.
- Use trainer clocks (plastic, wooden or card) to introduce the children to the term 'o'clock'. Look at the pictures on the display and help the children to assign times to them. For example: 'We eat breakfast at 8 o'clock'.
- Use photocopiable page 78 for some time-telling practice.

Creative development
- Using paper plates, split pins and strips of card, invite the children to make clock faces. Use them to show a given time.
- Ask the children to paint pictures of the things that they do during the day. Place the clocks that they made previously, showing the relevant times, under each painting.

Days of the week

*Learning objective: to introduce and name
the days of the week.*

What you need
The book *Mr Wolf's Week* by
Colin Hawkins (Heinemann
Young Books); coloured
backing paper; card;
paper; colouring
materials; adhesive
Velcro; border roll;
laminator or sticky-
backed plastic;
aprons; table covering.

What to do
Read *Mr Wolf's Week* to the
children. Talk about what the
wolf wears and what the
weather is like on the different
days. Discuss the number
and names of the days in
the week. Explain to the
children that they are
going to create a display about Mr
Wolf. Using the book as a guide
encourage seven children to draw an
outline of a wolf. Ask each child to
colour in their wolf using felt-tipped
pens. Laminate them.

Now, invite each child to draw an
appropriate set of clothes for their wolf,
taking care to match them in terms of
size. Ask the children to colour them in
and laminate the individual articles of
clothing.

Cover the display board in a bright
colour and use border roll to
make seven discrete sections,
each one containing a different
day. Once complete, staple a wolf
into each section and attach the
clothes with Velcro. At the top of
each section add the days of
the week with Velcro,
allowing opportunities
for the children to
develop their matching
skills.

Talk about
● What is your favourite
day of the week? Why?
How many days are in a
week? How many days are
in a weekend?
● What clothes do you wear
at the weekend? What
clothes do you wear during
the week? Are they different?
Which are your favourite clothes?

Home links
● Ask the children to find out from
their parents which day of the week
they were born on.
● Ask parents to teach their children
the days of the week.

MATHS

Using the display
Language and literacy
● Together, write an alternative to *Mr Wolf's Week*, to include something different for Mr Wolf to do each day.
● Challenge the children to write a list detailing different activities that they do each day.
● Make a collection of other stories, songs, poems and rhymes which centre around the days of the week. Make a display of them and share them with the children.

Mathematics
● Challenge the children to match and sequence the days of the week, asking them to name what day comes before and after a given day, or to suggest something that happens on a particular day.
● Make a block graph showing the days of the week that the children were born on. Which is the most popular day? Which is the least popular day?

Knowledge and understanding of the world
● Create a simple weekly weather chart for the children to record the changes in the weather using pictures. Extend this to incorporate symbols for different weather conditions.

● Hold up a weather symbol, and challenge an individual child to use the clothes to dress Mr Wolf appropriately.
● Provide a selection of materials for the children to test for warmth so Mr Wolf will not feel the cold.
● Talk about the dangers of too much sun. How can Mr Wolf protect himself from the sun?

Physical development
● Invite the children to play 'What's the time Mr Wolf?'. Choose a 'wolf' for the children to follow. The children call out, 'What's the time Mr Wolf?'. The wolf replies, for example 'One o'clock'. The children follow behind and repeat the process until the wolf surprises them with the words, 'DINNER TIME!' and chases them away. The wolf catches a child to take his place and the game continues.

Creative development
● Use fur fabric and other materials to create simple finger puppets of different animals. Use the puppets for story-telling and imaginative play.

All aboard!

*Learning objective: to
introduce months of the year
and pictorial representation.*

What you need
A variety of reclaimed boxes;
masking tape; glue; scissors;
paint; card; paintbrushes;
lollipop sticks; felt-tipped
pens; roll of white paper;
marker pens; pastels;
concentrated dye; corrugated
card; two computer labels for
each month of the year;
aprons; table covering.

What to do
Open out the boxes into
their net shapes and reseal with
masking tape to hide the
advertisements. Make twelve 'train
carriages' and an engine by painting the
boxes in a range of colours. Add wheels
and other features with card and paint.
Attach a different month label on the
side of each carriage and join them
together using strips of card to form a
long train. Make a train track using
strips of corrugated card and paint.
Invite a group of children to create
scenery using pastels, marker pens and
then covering with the dye.

Challenge each child to draw their
face onto a piece of card. Ask them to
attach their card 'face' onto a lollipop
stick. Invite the children to place the
stick into the relevant birthday carriage.

Talk about
● How many months are there in a
year? Can the children name them in
the correct order? Which month has
the most/least days?
● What month is your birthday in?
How many children have their birthday
in the same month as you? Which
month has the most birthdays?

Home links
● Ask parents to talk about family
birthdays with their child – which
months are they in? Talk about the
order of birthdays throughout the year
– who comes first, next and so on?

Further display table ideas
● Create a table-top display using
different implements for telling and
measuring the time.
● Use a collection of boxes of different
sizes and shapes with lids to fit on top
and objects to place inside.

Patterns

Building patterns

Learning objective: to make observations about the immediate environment.

What you need
Camera; printing materials; paint; paper; felt-tipped pens; coloured paper; scissors; glue; stapler; Cellophane; Velcro; straws; aprons; table covering.

What to do
Take a selection of photographs of patterns on buildings including brick, window and roof patterns. Show the children the photographs. Ask them to describe the patterns and to say where they can be seen.

Explain that you would like them each to choose one of the photographs and copy part of the pattern. Let them choose how they make the pattern – they may print, use coloured paper, Cellophane, straws, or rolled pieces of paper. Provide paper, paint, coloured paper, printing blocks, felt-tipped pens and glue for the children to use. Encourage the children to look closely at the photographs, think about the colours and shapes they will need and how the patterns repeat. When the patterns are completed, assemble them to create the effect of a patterned building. Laminate and attach Velcro to the back of some of the patterns and encourage the children to match them. Place the photographs around the display to demonstrate the inspiration for the patterns.

Talk about
● Look at the photographs together and develop the children's descriptive vocabulary by introducing words such as: vertical, horizontal, circular, diagonal, repeating and so on.
● Ask the children to describe the patterns to each other. Can their partner guess which building it can be found on? Which photograph corresponds to which pattern?
● Where else in the pictures can they see patterns? What sort of patterns do you like?

Home links
● Ask parents for permission to take the children on a walk around the local environment to look for 'building patterns'.
● Encourage parents to discuss patterns that are found in the children's own homes.

The visually stimulating topic of pattern provides great scope for colourful and exciting displays with potential for learning across the curriculum. In this chapter there are among others, ideas for exploring pattern in nature, in jewellery and around the home.

Patterns

THEMES ON DISPLAY
for early years

Flower power

Learning objective: to recognize and make patterns using nature as a stimulus.

What you need

Selection of cut and potted flowers (pictures may be used if not available); flowered objects such as fabric and pictures; magnifying glasses; light blue backing paper; paint; finger-paints; sponges; large sheets of coloured paper; everyday objects to print with including wheels; scissors; stapler; glue; coloured sticky paper; coloured card; green paper or Cellophane; coloured straws; reclaimed materials.

What to do

Arrange a display of the different flowers and flowered objects. Encourage the children to use magnifying glasses to look at the flowers for any patterns. Explain to them that there are two types of patterns on the flowers – repeating patterns and random patterns.

Explain that the children are going to make some large flowers for a display. Each of the flowers will be different in design and have different patterns.

Divide the children into small groups, give them some different-shaped 'petals' and set them the following tasks:
- *Group 1* – cut long thin petals from two shades of coloured paper, mix the paint in complementary colours. Show them how to use the wheels to make patterns with the paint on the petals.
- *Group 2* – cut circular petals from paper in two different colours, mix paint in complementary colours and let the children print on them using found objects.
- *Group 3* – cut small and large ovals in two colours. Show the children how to sponge-print using complementary colours.
- *Group 4* – let the children paint large sheets of card and add patterns with finger-paints to make a flower box.

Make a border by sticking strips of coloured sticky paper onto circles of card to create small flowers.

MATHS

Assemble the display by putting up the light blue backing paper and attaching the flower box by folding the card and stapling it to the wall. Arrange the three large patterned flowers above the flower box and add stems from green Cellophane or paper. Glue the small flowers around the edge to create a border. Attach labels saying – spiky petals, round petals, and so on.

Arrange some of the flowers and stimulus objects near to the display. Provide coloured straws, card and sticky paper for the children to make their own patterned flowers. Use reclaimed materials to make vases to arrange the flowers in.

Talk about
● Do you have any patterns on your clothes? Are they repeating patterns? What are your favourite colours in the patterns?
● Are there any patterns in your bedroom at home? Are there any in other rooms in your home? What makes a repeating pattern?

Home links
● Ask parents to talk about the colours, patterns, shapes and sizes of flowers that they see together when they are out.
● Ask parents to donate bulbs for the children to plant.

Using the display
Personal, social and emotional development
● Encourage the children's interest in living things by setting up a growing table. Ask two children to be responsible for it each day.
● Encourage the children to talk about the needs of growing plants – try to make links between this and their own growth.
● Ask children why they think people give each other flowers. Talk about how flowers are given for different occasions such as birthdays, christenings and anniversaries. Explain that people also send them sometimes to say 'sorry' or 'thank you'.

Language and literacy
● Play a guessing game whereby the children have to guess the flower on the display from its description.
● Work with children to make a non-fiction 'big book' about flowers. Where can they be found? What colours, shapes and sizes are they?

Mathematics
● Challenge the children to make patterned flowers using small construction materials such as Cleversticks. Using photocopiable page 79, ask them to try to copy the patterns using Cleversticks.
● Encourage the children to count the number of petals on each flower. Which has the most/least?

● Provide the children with a selection of coloured petals in different shapes to sort.

Knowledge and understanding of the world
● Talk about the different seasons and how flowers start to grow at specific times of the year.
● Investigate how flowers take up water by placing white flowers in coloured water. Ask the children to predict what will happen and to make observations and conclusions.

Creative development
● Make flowers that 'grow' by attaching a painted cardboard flower to a piece of dowelling and placing it through a plastic cup. Push the dowelling and watch the flower grow.
● Make individual flower cakes using a basic fairy cake mixture, coloured buttercream and a selection of small sweets. Challenge the children to make patterns on the small cakes.

Patterns

THEMES ON DISPLAY
for early years

Animal patterns

Learning objective: to recognize patterns on animals

What you need
White backing paper; oil pastels; drawing pencils; card; scissors; stapler; sponges; paint; newspaper; cold-water paste; cardboard tubes; crêpe and tissue paper; black paper; fishing wire; glue; selection of animal books and pictures; small-world animals; aprons; table covering.

What to do
Let the children examine and explore the books and pictures and encourage them to look for animal patterns. Which patterns do they recognize? Explain that they are going to create a display using animal patterns.

Use sponges to print leaf patterns onto large pieces of white paper in different shades of yellow and green. When dry, attach to the wall to use as backing paper. Roll and twist the newspaper and attach to cardboard tubes to create a tree trunk and branches. Mix the cold-water paste to a thin consistency, dip sheets of paper in paste and mould onto the tree trunk and branches to create a 'bark' effect. When dry, paint brown, adding leaves cut from crêpe, tissue and printed leaf pattern paper. Now attach to the display using fishing wire to ensure the branches are at different heights and angles.

Referring to the books and pictures, challenge the children to draw animals with patterns, such as zebras, leopards, giraffes, tigers, snakes and so on. Encourage them to use the oil pastels to add the patterns. When complete, add an outline, mount in black and cut out.

Arrange the animals on the display board to create a jungle scene. Place a table in front of the display to show the reference books and provide a selection of animals for sorting and counting activities.

Talk about
● Explain to the children that jaguars, cheetahs and leopards all belong to the cat family. They

MATHS

look similar and can all run fast and pounce, but when you look closely they have different markings on their fur.

● Talk about the animals on the display. What are their names? What do they look like? Can you describe how they move? What do they eat and where do they live?

● Discuss the differences between domestic, wild animals and animals held in captivity. Challenge the children to think of any

domestic animals with patterns – such as Dalmatians and tabby cats.

Home links

● Encourage parents to visit a zoo or farm with their children, paying particular attention to the names of the animals and their patterns.

● Suggest that parents visit the local library with their child and choose a relevant animal book to bring in and share with the group.

Using the display
Language and literacy

● Act as scribe, compiling a collection of words about the patterns on the animals such as, stripy, black and white, spotty and so on.

● Make up verses or poems about the different animals. Describe them, without mentioning their names and end with the words, 'What am I?'.

● Tell the children a selection of animal folk stories such as *The Greedy Zebra* by Mwenye Hadithi and Adrienne Kennaway (Hodder).

Mathematics

● Encourage the children to sort the collection of animals using the different patterns as the criteria.

● Ask the children to look at the display and estimate the number of animals in each group. Which group has the most and least numbers in? Count them. Were the children's guesses accurate?

● Count the number of animals on the display. Encourage the children to record the amounts of each animal, by drawing the animal and writing the correct number.

Knowledge and understanding of the world

● Consider climates in different places and how it affects animal and plant life.

● Help the children to find out about the different types of places where you can find animals such as jungles, deserts, the arctic and so on.

● Talk about the characteristics of particular animals and ask the children to suggest possible reasons for them. For example, ask the children why they think that giraffes have long necks, why lions have sharp teeth, why elephants have long trunks or why monkeys have long arms.

Physical development

● Use available large apparatus to create a 'jungle circuit' for the children to move under, over, around, between and so on. Invite the children to take on the role of being different animals in different sections of the circuit. For example: Can they prowl like lions? Can they slither like snakes? Can they stalk like tigers? Can they lumber along like elephants?

Creative development

● Make simple puppets using patterned fake animal fur, glue and felt for the features. Invite the children to name their puppet.

● Compose a piece of patterned music with the children by using percussion instruments in a recurring sequence. Extend this by drawing different scores for them to follow.

Spots and stripes

Learning objective: to recognize specific patterns such as spots and stripes.

What you need
The book *My Mum and Dad Make Me Laugh* by Nick Sharratt (Walker Books); paper; coloured paint; paintbrushes; sponge rollers; finger-paints; circles of gummed paper; tissue paper; glue; stapler; paper; Brusho (or watered-down paint and paintbrushes); table; coloured counters; Multilink; animal outlines; aprons; table covering.

What to do
Read the story to the children and explain that spots and stripes are different types of patterns. Discuss the characters in the story and explain that you are all going to make a display and of these characters.

To make the display wallpaper, choose two children to paint the striped wallpaper using the sponge rollers dipped into paint. Now choose two children to make the spotted wallpaper by colouring the paper using Brusho (or watered-down paint). Once dry, add finger-painted spots in a darker shade.

Choose a further two children to draw pictures of the Mum and Dad from the story. Ask them to add clothes to their pictures, painting the Mum with spots and the Dad with stripes. Now ask a child to draw a car adding painted stripes and puffed circles of tissue paper for the spots.

Staple the Mum and Dad in front of the relevant section of 'wallpaper' and position the car in the centre. Fold strips of paper, concertina-style, asking the children to draw stripes and spots alternately. Use this as a border and complete the display by adding labels and interactive questions.

Place a table in front of the display with the story book, drawings of vehicles, animals and people with spotted and striped patterns, coloured counters and Multilink.

Talk about
● Ask the children to suggest words to label the display. Explain to the children that stripes going up and down are called vertical; across are called horizontal and on a slant are called diagonal.

Home links
● Ask parents to bring in oddments of wallpaper and set up a 'wallpaper shop'.

Using the display
Personal, social and emotional development
● Ask the children how they would feel if they were poorly and covered in spots. Ask them to tell you about times when they may have had 'chicken-pox' or other spots.
● In small groups, ask the children to work co-operatively and take it in turns to draw the different parts of a patterned animal.

Language and literacy
● Make a simple book of 's' words and pictures encouraging the children to be the authors and illustrators.
● Model simple story writing with the children, based around the adventures of a spotted monster. Include where he came from, his name, what he was like and what mischief he got up to!
● Ask the children to tell you about the things that make them laugh. Why do they find them funny?

Mathematics
● Challenge the children to describe the patterns, encouraging them to use the correct vocabulary.

● Devise a questionnaire for the children to use to find out which is the most popular pattern in the group. Put this information into a bar graph.
● Use Multilink to create tower patterns. Help the children to understand how to make repeating patterns and encourage them to use the relevant vocabulary.

Knowledge and understanding of the world
● Explain to the children that spots and stripes can be found on flags. Tell them that each country has a different flag. Show them a variety of flags and talk about the colours and patterns. Let them design their own flag.

Creative development
● Look closely at some of the paintings by Paul Klee which contain a range of coloured stripes. Invite the children to use strips of coloured tissue paper to create their own work in a similar style.
● Provide materials with spots and stripes in different colours and sizes and encourage the children to use them to create their own collages.

How many elephants?

Learning objective: to learn about patterns of growth.

What you need

Card; black and white powder paint; paintbrushes; thick wool; copy of the rhyme 'Elephants come out to play' on photocopiable page 80; pictures or books containing elephants; adhesive Velcro; sticky labels; laminator or sticky-backed plastic; blue backing paper; stapler; scissors; aprons; table covering.

What to do

Introduce the rhyme to the children, asking them to say what animals are mentioned. What do they look like? What colour are they? How many are there? Explain to the children that they are going to make a big display of the rhyme for them to use. Together, look at some pictures of elephants and ask the children how they think they might draw them. Encourage them to draw a big, round body, a round head, a curly trunk, a short, stumpy tail and four short legs. Once complete, provide them with black and white powder paint to experiment making grey. Use the paint to paint five grey elephants.

Once dry, add a sticky label to each one. Ask the children to write the numbers from 1 to 5 onto the labels. Cover the elephants in sticky-backed plastic, or laminate them

Staple the backing paper to the display board and use the wool to make a large spider's web shape. Attach Velcro to the back of the elephants and to the spider's web. Word process the rhyme, make into a booklet with one verse on each page and attach the corresponding numbered elephant on the opposite page with Velcro.

To enable the rhyme booklet to be read when all the elephants have been taken out of the booklet and stuck onto the web, invite the children to draw the appropriate number of elephants under the removable elephant.

Place or hang the booklet near to the display for everyone to see.

THEMES ON DISPLAY
for early years

Talk about

● Explain to the children that there are two main types of elephant – the African elephant and the Indian elephant. Tell the children that Indian elephants have smaller ears than African elephants.

● Talk to the children about what they have seen or would expect to see on a web. Explain to them that a spider spins fine silvery threads to make a web as it moves. They make their webs to catch small insects to eat.

● What shapes and patterns can the children see in the web? Where would they expect to see one?

Using the display

Personal, social and emotional development

● Make the rhyme into a circle game by substituting a child's name instead of an elephant, who then walks around the circle. Repeat this, calling another name to join the first child, and so on.

● Ask the children to tell you about their favourite game. What are the rules and how many can play?

Language and literacy

● Read *The Very Busy Spider* by Eric Carle (Hamish Hamilton) to the children.

● Make up new rhymes using a similar structure. Substitute the type of animal and the place where they are playing.

● Focus on key words from the rhyme asking the children to suggest alternatives, for example, 'called' could be substituted by 'shouted', 'shrieked', 'yelled' and so on.

● Read the story *Sarah the Spider* by Hilary Robinson and Jane Abbbott (Belitha Press). Ask the children to discuss Sarah's character.

Mathematics

● Encourage the children to place the elephants in sequence both forwards and backwards.

● Use other traditional rhymes, such as, 'Ten fat sausages', to introduce or reinforce larger numbers.

● Do some practical subtraction by taking a different number of elephants off the spider's web each time.

Home links

● Provide copies of the rhyme for the children to take home and share with their families.

● Ask parents to reinforce counting to five with their child while they are either at home or out and about.

Knowledge and understanding of the world

● Discuss with the children where different animals live. Would you really find elephants on a spider's web?

● Use the spider's web to help develop simple mapping techniques. Start at the centre and ask a child to direct an elephant to a specific part of the web – for example, move down the web; stop; move to the left; stop and so on.

Physical development

● Tell the children to find a partner – one child should be a spider, the other an elephant. Challenge them to take on the correct shape and position to move around a large space, either quickly or slowly.

Creative development

● Provide plastic straws for the children to lay on the sand, making paths and webs. Encourage them to move elephants and spiders around the paths, playing as they travel.

● Let the children use reclaimed materials to create a playground that the elephants would enjoy.

Patterns

THEMES ON DISPLAY
for early years

Patchwork patterns

Learning objective: to create individual patterns using different media.

What you need
Two large pieces of plain cotton fabric; smaller triangles of cotton fabric; oil pastels; diluted fabric dye; spray bottles; card; white backing paper; paint; string; sponges; PVA glue; permanent black markers; empty cereal boxes; wax crayons; small pieces of dowelling; masking tape; Brusho (or paintbrushes and watered-down paint); construction kit such as Lego; Multilink; straws; sticky tape; Blu-Tack; reclaimed materials; aprons; floor covering; table; books and pictures showing harbour scenes; picture book *Window* by Jeannie Baker (Red Fox).

What to do
Look through the *Window* book together, discussing how the view changes. What things can the children see? What would they like to see from their window? Ask the children to

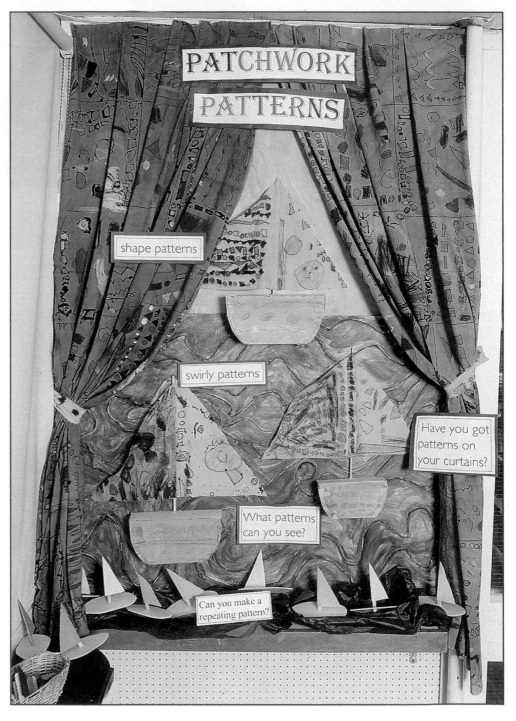

imagine that they live close to the water. What things would they see when they looked out of their window?

Begin the display by thinking about the inside of the window and the patterns that can be seen on curtains. Divide the two large pieces of fabric into squares, using the black marker. In each section, invite the children to draw patterns using the marker pen. Then ask them to colour the patterns using oil pastels. When all the sections are complete (and the children have gone home) lay the fabric on the covered floor and spray with diluted fabric dye, leave to dry over night.

Draw patterns on the triangles of fabric and follow the same procedure to create the sails for the boats. Make the boats by turning cereal boxes inside out, cutting them to shape, and rejoining with masking tape. Invite the children to draw patterns on these with wax crayons and cover with Brusho or watered-down paint.

To create the water for the display, encourage the children to glue pieces of string onto a large sheet of card to form a wave pattern. When dry, paint over this with blue paint mixed with glue to give a shiny effect. Use pale blue paint to sponge-print the sky onto some white backing paper.

To assemble the display, staple the sky and sea to the display board and 'hang' the curtains. Attach the sails to the boats using dowelling and strong glue and position in the sea to form a pattern. Place Multilink, construction kits and reclaimed materials on a nearby table and encourage the children to make some boats. Ask them to place the finished products on the 'window sill' (or table underneath the display). Provide straws, sticky tape, paper, Blu-Tack and colouring materials for the children to make and attach sails to their boats.

Talk about
● Why do boats need sails? Do all boats have sails? What makes the boat move? Have you ever been on a boat?
● Discuss with the children that boats have different purposes. Explain that some carry passengers and vehicles and others carry cargo. Tell the children that the front of the boat is called the bow,

the rear is called the stern, the left side is known as port, and the right as starboard.

Home links
● Ask parents to send in any toy boats for use in the water tray.
● Ask parents to talk with their child about patterns at home, such as on carpets, wallpaper, crockery, upholstery and so on.

Using the display
Language and literacy
● Challenge the children to take turns to commentate on a boat race. Encourage them to describe each boat in detail, paying particular attention to the patterns. They should decide which boat would come first, second and so on.
● Devise sentences involving the boat and its colour. Work together to come up with some simple rhymes, such as 'The boat is green, it is beautiful and clean'.

Mathematics
● Ask the children to count and number the boats in the sea. Which boat is the biggest? Which boat is the smallest?
● Challenge the children to solve simple problems such as 'If there were two people in each boat, how many people would there be all together?'; 'If there were three people in the boat and one fell over board, how many would be left in the boat?'. Repeat using different number combinations.

Knowledge and understanding of the world
● Investigate floating and sinking with the children. Provide a range of objects for them to predict and test which will float or sink.
● Use construction equipment to make simple boats, asking the children to name and label the various parts.

Creative development
● Change the role-play area into a boat or canal barge using corrugated card and decorating with brightly-coloured flowers and patterns.
● Make small boats using pieces of polystyrene, straws, paper and colouring materials. Test which boat floats the best in the water tray.
● Make a collection of tins, metal jugs and pots for the children to paint and decorate with bright patterns.

Jewellery patterns

Learning objective: to recognize and make a variety of patterns.

What you need
Table-top covered with a dark fabric; selection of beads, buttons, cotton reels, different-coloured and shaped pastas (threadable); laces in different sizes and colours; range of storage baskets; examples of beaded necklaces; self-drying clay; oil pastels; thick card; coloured card; acrylic and metallic paint; sequins; glitter; glue; reclaimed boxes and tubes; colouring materials; piece of dowelling; hair clips; laminator or sticky-backed plastic; table covering; aprons.

attach to hair clips with strong glue to make brooches. Add patterns with glitter to pre-cut card in bracelet shapes. Make rings from card using metallic paint and sequins to create patterns. Make display containers by painting and adding features to reclaimed boxes.

Now make some activity cards that show different designs for necklaces and bracelets using the available materials. Include a variety of patterns on the card, such as circular, straight and recurring patterns.

Make patterns with the children by threading beads onto a lace. Once complete, show them how the pattern remains constant even though its shape can be changed, for example by making the lace into a circle, oval or wiggly line.

Encourage the children to model their finished jewellery. Keep the children's favourite combinations and display them. Invite them to draw and record their creations using writing and drawing materials.

Talk about
● Talk to the children about their necklaces. Ask them to describe their patterns. How many colours have they used? Does the pattern reach the end? How could they make their design better?

What to do
Talk about different types of jewellery, such as beads, brooches and necklaces. Explain to the children that many pieces of jewellery are highly patterned.

Provide self-drying clay and encourage the children to mould bead shapes. Help them to make a centre hole with a piece of dowelling. When dry, paint in bright colours with acrylic paint.

Cut shapes from card and ask the children to colour them in with oil pastels to form a pattern. Laminate and

Home links
● Ask parents to supply old beaded necklaces for display or for taking apart to make into new necklaces.

Further display table ideas
● Set up a music table with a selection of percussion instruments. Suggest that the children make up musical patterns of their own and provide drawing materials for them to record their patterns.

Shapes

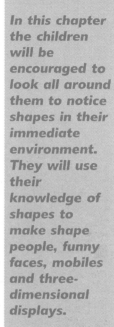
Find a shape

Learning objective: to recognize and begin to name large shapes.

What you need
Backing paper; paint; sponges; stapler; paintbrushes; large white paper; felt-tipped pens; sticky-backed plastic; non-permanent marker pens; scissors.

What to do
Staple the white paper to the display board, covering the bottom half with sticky-backed plastic. Use a sponge to print the blue sky. Explain to the children that they are going to go for a walk outside to find as many different-sized shapes as possible. Reinforce the names and introduce the properties of common shapes to help the children on their search. When you return from the walk. Encourage the children to use large pieces of white paper to draw and paint a picture containing some of the shapes they saw on their walk – for example a house with rectangles for windows.

Use a felt-tipped pen to emphasize the shapes in the pictures, cut out and attach to the display board to create an outdoor scene. Allow the children to use the marker pen to add finishing touches such as lines on the road. These can be altered by wiping the surface clean and starting again. Label the names of the shapes on the display.

Talk about
● Ask the children to tell you about the shapes of windows in their own homes. Are they always rectangles? How can you tell the difference between a square and a rectangle?

Home links
● Ask parents to join the shape walk, to help spot specific shapes.
● Ask parents to discuss the shapes found around their homes.

In this chapter the children will be encouraged to look all around them to notice shapes in their immediate environment. They will use their knowledge of shapes to make shape people, funny faces, mobiles and three-dimensional displays.

Shape friends

Learning objective: to recognize and name common 2-D shapes.

What you need
Four large, strong cardboard tubes; thick card; backing paper; large coloured card; variety of fabric and papers; paint; paintbrushes; scissors; glue; stapler; split pins; household materials such as rubber gloves, dusters, scourers; selection of shapes and everyday objects in a range of shapes; aprons; table covering.

What to do
Cut four pieces of card the same height as the tubes. Cover the tubes and the card with brightly-coloured backing paper. Staple the card to the tubes to form a frame ready to attach the completed 'shape friends'.

Show the four-sided frame to the children and explain that they are going to decorate the frame with people made from shapes such as circles, rectangles, squares and triangles.

Talk about how the children would make their 'shape friends' and give the children the opportunity to experiment practically, in groups, with a given shape in different sizes.

Cut large shapes from coloured card for each 'friend' – ensuring that each has all its body parts and will fit onto the frame. Let the children work in small groups to cover the body parts using a range of techniques such as cutting out fabric and paper into different-sized shapes or gluing and printing with different sized shapes.

To create facial features cut household materials into shapes and back on card. Attach these to the heads with Velcro

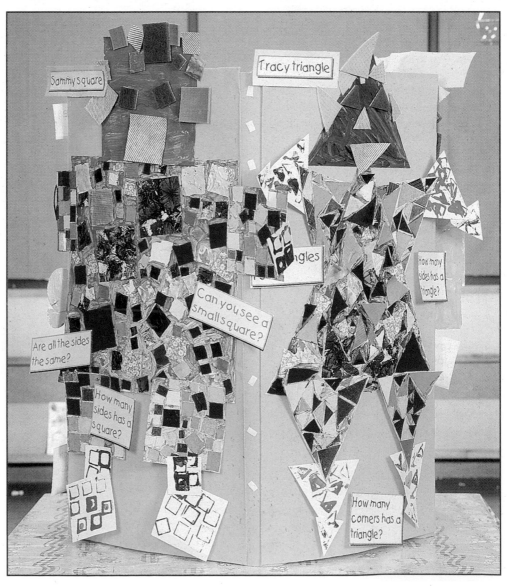

and store on the tubes when not in use. Once they are complete join the body parts with split pins and attach to the frame.

Talk about
● Talk about the different 'shape friends' with the children. What shapes can you see? Why are there squares inside the square body? What colours can you see? Can you see any patterns? What parts of the body can you move on our 'shape friends'?

● What shall we call our 'shape friends'? How can you be a good friend? What does a friend do? How many 'shape friends' have we made?

Home links
● Explain to parents that the children have been making shape people. Ask them to make a shape face with their children at home, using household objects. Ask the children to bring them in and display them alongside the 'shape friends' display.

Using the display
Personal, social and emotional development
● Ask the children to tell you who their friends are. What games do they play together? Could they play with more children to make new friends?
● Establish a 'meeting place' in the role-play area. Encourage the children to talk to new friends in the 'meeting place', finding out as much information as possible, such as their likes and dislikes, families and so on.

Language and literacy
● Challenge the children to label the parts of the body, either using emergent writing or by acting as scribe for them.
● Provide the children with a think bubble outline. Ask them to write or draw the thoughts of the 'shape friends'.

Mathematics
● Familiarize the children with the properties of the different shapes by asking the children to close their eyes and feel the shapes. Can they guess what the shapes are? How do they know?
● Encourage the children to use a set of shapes to make a face.

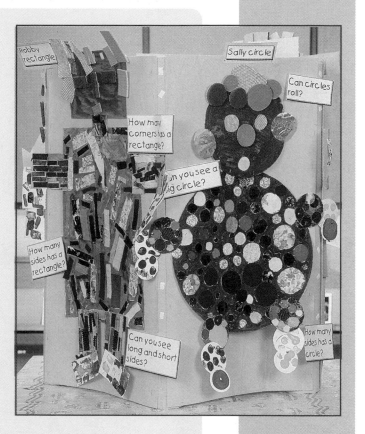

Knowledge and understanding of the world
● Discuss the different body parts, where they are joined, and how they move.
● Discuss what makes us different to the shape people on the display.
● Talk about living things and their characteristics such as breathing, moving, eating and so on. Provide a selection of objects to sort into sets of 'living' and 'non-living'.

Creative development
● Challenge the children to create other objects to accompany the 'shape friends' such as shape toys, vehicles, houses and so on.
● Make moveable card families by attaching body parts with split pins. Decorate with fabric, wool and paint to create features. Attach to sticks to create simple puppets. Work together to make up a story where the children can use the puppets to develop their speaking and listening skills.

What goes around?

Learning objective: to recognize and name a given shape.

What you need
Coloured backing paper; pencil; string; stapler; scissors; washing-up liquid; bubble-blowers; red and yellow paint; finger-paints; straw; shallow container; white and coloured paper; card; laminator or sticky-backed plastic; glue; compass; magazines; felt-tipped pens.

What to do
Introduce the shape of a circle through sorting activities and by discussing the properties of circles. Explain that lots of things around us are circular in shape. Show the children one or two examples from around the room. Explain to them that they are going to make a display just about circles.

Staple the backing paper onto the display board and use a pencil and string to draw a large circle onto a piece of bright paper (if necessary this could be completed in two halves). Attach the circle to the display board.

Now provide the children with a selection of coloured magazines. Ask them to look through the magazines and find examples of pictures with circles such as a car, washing machine and so on. Encourage the children to draw pictures of the objects that they found with circles. When the pictures have been coloured in, provide the children with circles cut from coloured paper and suggest that they glue the paper circles onto their drawings in the appropriate places.

Mix the washing-up liquid with paint and give the children the opportunity to use the bubble-blowers.. Take prints of the bubbles by gently laying paper on top of them.

Assemble the display by making a border using black circles and bubble prints cut to shape. Use finger-paint to create a title by printing the outline of the letters. Once dry, cut out the letters, leaving a thin, white border. Mount the letter shapes onto overlapping coloured circles.

Mount the children's pictures onto black paper, arrange and staple onto the large circle. Fold a large sheet of brightly-coloured card to make a shelf and staple to the wall below the circle. Cut rings and arrows from

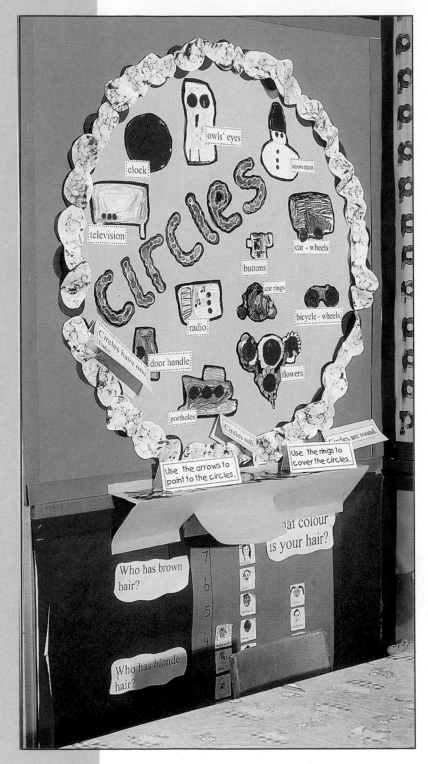

coloured card and laminate, place these on the shelf and invite the children to use them to identify the circles on the display. To complete the display, make appropriate hand-written or word-processed labels.

Talk about
● Discuss with the children the shapes of their buttons. Are all buttons always round? What other fasteners can you get? What shape are they? Are buttons always the same size?

Home links
● Ask parents to send in any odd buttons for the children to use for sorting activities or to make circle pictures with.
● Ask parents to look through some magazines with their child. Can they find any objects with circles in them?

Using the display
Personal, social and emotional development
● Teach the children a range of traditional circle games such as 'There's a little sandy girl'; 'The farmer's in his dell' or 'In and out the dusty bluebells', all in *This Little Puffin* compiled by Elizabeth Matterson (Puffin).
● Provide circular biscuits, buttercream and a selection of sweets. Ask the children to decorate them for their friends. Sit in a circle together to share and eat them.

Language and literacy
● Make a list with the children of all the objects that they can think of that are circular or contain circles.
● Take all the labels off the display and challenge the children to place them in alphabetical order.
● Ask the children to group together all the objects that start with the same sound. Let them use the arrows for this activity.

Mathematics
● Ask the children to use Blu-Tack to place the rings and arrows to highlight the circles on the display.
● Count the circles on each object and ask the children to write the numbers, and attach them to the appropriate objects.

Knowledge and understanding of the world
● Let the children use magnifying glasses to examine the bubbles closely. Encourage them to look closely at the colours and shapes of each one.
● Why do the children think wheels are round? Would any other shapes work? What shapes wouldn't work well? Why?

Creative development
● Make a variety of coloured bubble prints and use them to create new pictures when they are dry.
● Provide strips of coloured tissue paper for the children to hold and swirl, making circles in the air above, below and behind them. Put the moves to music and make into a circle dance.

Shape windows

Learning objective: to recognize and name properties of common 2-D shapes.

What you need
Selection of shapes; set rings; coloured card; string; ribbon; glue; scissors; white A4 paper and card; black border strips; paint; shapes to print with; drawing materials; stapler; small pre-cut squares, triangles, rectangles and circles.

What to do
Place the shapes and set rings on a table for the children to sort. When sorted by shape, ask them to name the shapes and anything special they notice about them, such as – it rolls, it has three sides and three points and so on.

Provide each child with one shape drawn on A4 paper and challenge the children to make it into a picture, for example a circle made into a pond, a car or a pair of glasses.

Cut out a large circle, rectangle, square and triangle from brightly-coloured card and double-mount onto pieces of white or cream coloured card. Attach the large shapes to the display board to make windows. Explain to the children that they are now going to make their own shapes in lots of different ways to fill the shape windows.

Let the children complete the following activities:
● Use shapes and coloured paint to print triangle shapes onto paper triangles. Mount the printed paper triangles onto pieces of triangular card.
● Make 'dot-to-dot' shapes on card and challenge the children to glue ribbon or

string to join the dots and complete the shape.

● Provide the children with pre-made frames of different-sized shapes, and matching small pre-cut shapes. Ask the children to stick the shapes around the frame to create a pattern.

As the children complete the activities, reinforce the properties of the various shapes using appropriate mathematical language such as corner, side, long, short and pointed.

Assemble the display as shown, by attaching the relevant shape pictures inside the large shape windows. Divide the display board into four sections with black border strips.

Talk about
● What picture did you make your shape into? Did you add any other shapes? Are the shapes big or small?
● Talk about the properties of each shape. Which shapes have four sides? Which shapes have three sides? How many corners does each shape have? Is there a link between the number of sides and the number of corners?

Home links
● Encourage the children to look at the shapes of their doors and windows. Ask them to draw pictures of them and bring them in to show each other.

Using the display
Personal, social and emotional development
● Make some sandwiches in different shapes and discuss the need for healthy eating and hygiene.

Language and literacy
● Encourage the children to write the name of the shape along each of its sides, to reinforce the different shapes' properties.
● Either scribe for or encourage the children to write a description of the pictures they made from a shape. Make the descriptions into a book to hang by the display.

Mathematics
● Provide the children with a large shape and a selection of smaller shapes to fit into it (tessellate). Discuss which shapes fit together easily. Why is this?
● Reinforce the differences between a rectangle and a square, by comparing the different lengths of ribbon or string used to make the dot-to-dot shapes.

Physical development
● Challenge the children to draw the shapes in the sand tray using a range of tools such as a straw, paintbrush or pencil. Which is the easiest shape to draw and why?
● Make a large shape using skipping ropes and suggest that the children follow the shape with bikes, prams or on foot.

Funny faces!

Learning objective: to recognize and use common 2-D shapes.

What you need
White and coloured card; plastic hoop; balsa wood; triangles of strong card; colouring materials; selection of various sized 2-D shapes; coloured card shapes of different shapes and sizes; fishing wire; glue; scissors; stapler; copies of paintings of faces by various artists such as Picasso.

What to do
Show the children the selection of pictures showing painted faces. Talk about the the shapes and features shown. Challenge them to make a face using the 2-D shapes. Introduce the names and properties of the shapes. Let them practice making different faces and then provide a large card shape

each. Challenge the children to use this shape as the head and to use the coloured card shapes to make the features on their 'funny' face. Refer to the portraits by famous painters and discuss the shapes used as they work.

Once completed, use balsa wood and the strong cardboard triangles to make square, rectangular and triangular frames. Attach the funny faces to the frames and hoop using fishing wire. Hang from the ceiling with the fishing wire. Attach labels giving information about the shapes and their properties.

Talk about
● Which shape makes the funniest face? How many shapes can you count on your face? Is the hair spiky or flat?

Home links
● Ask parents to help their child to collect pictures of faces from magazines to use for sorting or collage work.

MATHS

Using the display

Personal, social and emotional development
● Choose children to use facial expressions to show their emotions such as anger, fear, happiness, disappointment, excitement and so on.

Language and literacy
● Challenge the children to invent names for their 'funny face'. Introduce the idea of alliteration such as Tina or Tommy Triangle.
● Use the 'funny face' characters to stimulate some shared writing. Make suggestions for the characters – perhaps they are visiting a 'shape circus' or going on a 'shape journey'. Discuss the adventures or problems they might encounter.

Mathematics
● Hang numbers from each of the 'funny faces' to determine how many of each shape are hanging.

Knowledge and understanding of the world
● Talk about 'identikits'. Explain that they are used by the police to make up the face of a criminal.

● Provide the children with unbreakable mirrors for them to carefully study their own faces, paying close attention to the shape of the face, colour, hair-style, size and shape of nose, eyes, chin and mouth.

Physical development
● Use card, egg boxes, kitchen rolls, scissors, glue and ribbon to make monster masks with the children. Use them for imaginative play and drama work.
● Provide the children with self-drying clay and a range of shapes to press into it. Challenge the children to create a face tile by using the different shapes. Paint and varnish the finished products.

Creative development
● Encourage the children to create paintings or drawings in the style of Picasso. Mount and display these in a special exhibition for parents to come and view!
● Provide the children with magazines and newspapers and suggest that they cut out facial features. Encourage them to arrange and stick them on pieces of paper to create new faces.

THEMES ON DISPLAY for early years

Build a shape

Learning objective: to recognize, name and make common 3-D shapes.

What you need
Glue; scissors; card; stapler; felt-tipped pens; glue; paper; collage materials; coloured fabric; fishing wire; small cup hooks; backing paper; cubes, cuboids and cylinders to colour; selection of 3-D shapes; large pieces of card to make nets for the different shapes.

What to do
Show the children the selection of 3-D shapes and ask them to decide how they will sort them. Can they explain why they have sorted them in that way? If the children need help, suggest that they sort them into specific shapes and name the various properties of them, explaining that each side of the shape is called a face. Explain to the children that they are going to decorate cubes, cuboids and cylinders of different sizes, by drawing faces on them.

Draw nets of various sizes for each of the 3-D shapes onto card and photocopy them, enlarging and reducing the size to provide a variety of sizes and shapes. Make three big nets, one of each shape and invite individual children to draw 'faces' onto the shapes, adding hair and facial features using paper, collage materials and colours. Try to give each shape different features by using different combinations of colour, shape and style. Assemble the nets using glue, leaving a 'lid' on each one. Let the rest of the children use the smaller nets to colour and add facial features and hair to. Assemble the nets using glue and lots of patience! Remind the children of the properties of the individual shapes.

To create a backdrop ask the children to colour drawings of cubes, cuboids and cylinders. Cut out and mount in towers onto the backing paper.

Attach the fabric to the wall to give a ruched effect. Staple the towers of coloured shape drawings into three areas and screw the cup hooks into the

ceiling. Attach the fishing wire to the large 3-D shapes, fill with the smaller shapes and hook on to the cup hooks ensuring the 3-D shape hangs in front of the matching backdrop.

Talk about
● What shapes are the big shapes made up from? What similarities and differences can you see in the small shapes?
● What shapes do you think will be found in the large shape? How many small shapes does the large shape hold?

Home links
● Ask parents to talk to their children about the different-shaped packages that sweets can be found in.
● Encourage parents to collect empty 3-D packaging to send in to be used for junk modelling. Suggest that they name the shapes of the boxes and materials with their children.

Using the display

Personal, social and emotional development
● Make 'kindness cubes'. Ask the children to draw a picture of how they will be kind and place it in a decorated cube.

Language and literacy
● Write a letter as though it is from one of the 'shape faces'. Ask the children to write a letter back.
● Use cubes to make a selection of different purposeful dice. For example, make a dice to reinforce initial letter sounds (with a different sound on each face) or a set of dice to consolidate work on three letter words (two dice containing consonants and one with vowel sounds).
● Work with the children to create some simple shape poems. Write the finished poems onto the outside of the shapes.

Mathematics
● Ask the children to sort the small cubes, cylinders and cuboid faces into sets using a range of criteriam, such as hair colour and eye colour.
● Use the shape faces to create a pattern, changing one criteria at a time.

Physical development
● Make a range of construction kits containing cubes, cylinders and cuboids accessible to the children. Ask the children to use the shapes to make a scene such as a farmyard, a row of houses, an airport and so on.
● Challenge the children to work in pairs to pretend to be a 'jack-in-the-box'. One child should close the lid and wind the handle to make the other child jump out of the box!

Creative development
● Obtain a large box in the shape of a cube or cuboid – use this as a prop for a drama activity. Ask the children to come up with possible suggestions as to what may be inside the box or what it could be used for.

Shape shopping

Learning objective: to recognize, sort and match 3-D shapes.

What you need
Large picnic or shopping basket; food boxes and tins in different shapes and sizes; card; paper; felt-tipped pens; sticky tape; glue; Blu-Tack; set rings; cardboard stand; fabric to cover the table-top.

What to do
Cut pieces of paper to fit the cylinder-, cube- and cuboid-shaped items.

Encourage the children to draw pictures of different foods to glue onto the 3-D shapes to replace the original labels.

Choose a child to draw a large picture of a lady with a speech bubble. Cut her out and stick her to the cardboard stand.

Cover the table with fabric and arrange the 'food' in and around the basket. Position the lady near to the basket of food.

Place paper and writing materials near to the display for the children to write or draw the lady's words. Encourage them to stick the words onto the speech bubble with Blu-Tack.

Talk about
● When the children go shopping, what do they carry the shopping in? Which is their favourite food in the basket? Do they know anything else that is carried in a basket? What shape packaging do cornflakes come in? Which is the most popular shape packaging. Why?

Home links
● Encourage parents to reinforce the names of the 3-D shapes with their child by, for example, asking them to pick a certain shaped packet off the shelf, at home or at the shops.
● Ask parents to write or draw shopping lists with their children. Encourage them to bring the lists in and attach them to the display. Can they collect the things on the lady's list?

Further display table ideas
● Place 2-D shapes, set rings, card cut to various shapes and sizes and examples of shape pictures for the children to arrange, sort and use.
● Provide a wide selection of different sized and shaped containers. Leave the biggest containers with one face open. Ask the children to sort the remaining shapes and decide which container they could fit inside.

What can you see?

Colour the objects correctly.

Colour boxes

Cut out the shaded area and cover with coloured Cellophane. Cut around the outline and make the shape.

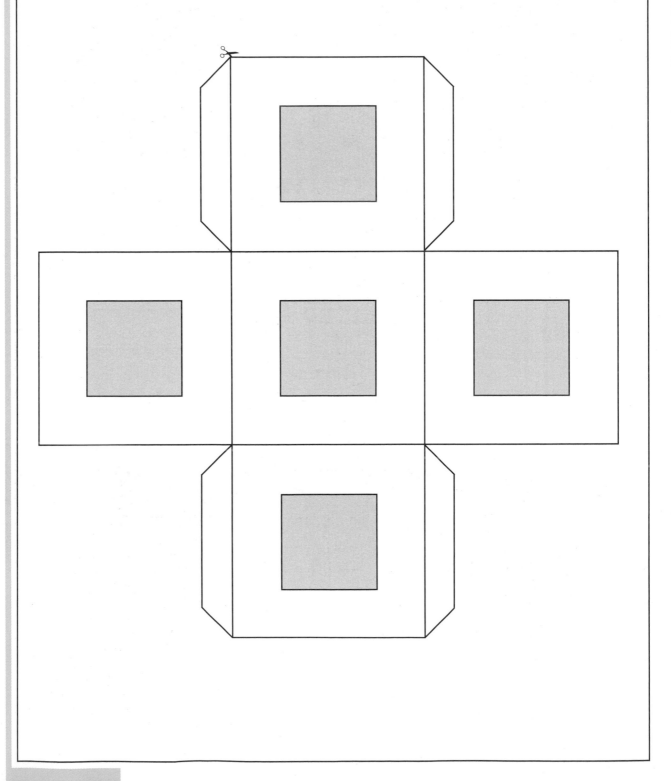

MATHS

Which teddy?

Draw lines to join the matching teddies.

Cake designs

Finish the patterns on the cakes.

Monkey babies

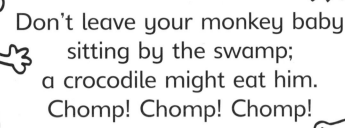

Don't leave your monkey baby
sitting by the swamp;
a crocodile might eat him.
Chomp! Chomp! Chomp!

Don't leave your monkey baby
sitting under the trees;
a snake might wrap him up.
Squeeze! Squeeze! Squeeze!

Don't leave your monkey baby
sitting by the track;
a lion might be lurking.
Snack! Snack! Snack!

Keep your monkey baby
high up in the trees.
Feed him on bananas.
Help pick off his fleas.

© Irene Rawnsley and John Foster

What time is it?

Cut out the pictures. Stick them under the correct clocks.

 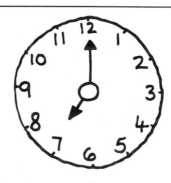

8 o'clock

12 o'clock

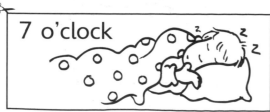 

7 o'clock

5 o'clock

Photocopiable

MATHS

What a picture!

Follow the code to colour the petals.

| 1 - red |
| 2 - blue |
| 3 - yellow |

Elephants come out to play

One elephant went out to play,
Upon a spider's web one day,
He was having such enormous fun,
That he called for another elephant to come.

Two elephants went out to play,
Upon a spider's web one day,
They were having such enormous fun,
That they called for another elephant to come.

Three elephants went out to play,
Upon a spider's web one day,
They were having such enormous fun,
That they called for another elephant to come.

Four elephants went out to play,
Upon a spider's web one day,
They were having such enormous fun,
That they called for another elephant to come.

Five elephants went out to play,
Upon a spider's web one day,
They were having such enormous fun,
That they called for another elephant to come.

(Traditional)

MATHS